HOW TO LEARN
FROM
A COURSE IN MIRACLES

How to Learn
from
A
COURSE
IN
MIRACLES

Third Edition

TARA SINGH

HarperSanFrancisco
A Division of HarperCollinsPublishers

THIRD EDITION
ORIGINALLY PUBLISHED IN 1985 BY LIFE ACTION PRESS.

Library of Congress Cataloging-in-Publication Data

Singh, Tara, 1919-
How to learn from A course in miracles.
1. Foundation for Inner Peace. Course in Miracles.
2. New Age movement.   3. Spiritual life.   I. Title.
BP605.N48F68 Suppl.3 1988   299'.93   87-21494
ISBN 1-55531-144-X (lim. ed.)
ISBN 1-55531-139-3 (pbk.)

ISBN 0-06-250781-8 (pbk.)
     92 93 94 MAPLE 10 9 8 7 6 5 4 3 2

This book is dedicated to the twenty: Lucille Frappier, Charles Johnson, Aliana Scurlock, Johanna Macdonald, Frank Nader, Clio Dixon, Richleigh and Kris Heagh, John, Acacia, and Crystal Williams, Jim Cheatham, Connie Willcuts, Norah Ryan, Ted Ward, Rachel Logel, Sandra Lewis, Nancy Marsh, Selina Scheer, and Richard Michael.

CONTENTS

THE WILL OF GOD

There is a silence and a certainty
Apart from time; a peace and quietness
Surrounded by a thousand angels' wings,
And kept inviolate by God's Own Hand.
It is for everyone. Yet very few
Have found it. It will wait for everyone
Who seek, and all of them will find at last
This secret haven, hidden from the world,
And yet in open sight. Its clarity
Is blazing, yet it is not often seen.
Its call is constant, yet is rarely heard.
Attack must overlook it, yet to love
It gives an instant answer. Here the Will
Of God is recognized and cherished still.
And it is here that finally God's Son
Will understand his will and God's are one.*

*This poem is from *The Gifts Of God* by the Scribe of *A Course In Miracles*. It is an incomparable book of poetry containing some of the most important words ever spoken.

INTRODUCTION TO THE
SECOND EDITION

A MAN WHO HAS discovered his inner calling can no longer be bought and sold. He has the voice of his own conviction and is not regulated by external circumstances. He is energized and eternally grateful for a productive and meaningful life; his function relates him with Eternal Laws. Inner calling, having its own vitality of action and wisdom, brings him to consistency at all levels of his being. And it is this consistency that allows self-honesty in his life.

The action of one's inner calling begins with responsibility. In me, it began with the commitment to directly discover whether *A Course In Miracles*[1] could be brought into application. Coming into contact with the Course had brought with it a sense of responsibility I had never known before. Responsibility demands consistency. This undertaking energized me and led to the discovery that responsibility has its own source of energy. The urgency of its authentic action brought me to the clarity that I must give my whole attention to each lesson of the Course.

I moved to a solitary place for an extended period to study the Course. It seemed as if I had been prepared for the entry of the Course upon these planes and to be a part of its extension. Instantly, I discovered the energy "celestial speed-up"[2] imparts to bring order in life. One is constantly freed from involvements, as if ordained to become part of universal order.

The impact of:

> *Nothing real can be threatened.*
> *Nothing unreal exists.*[3]

set my mind aflame. They were the most powerful words I had ever heard. Their explosion undermined everything else. These Eternal Words — Absolute and all-encompassing — silenced part of the chatter of the brain in me forever.

From Lesson One,

> *Nothing I see...means anything.*[4]

to Lesson Ten,

> *My thoughts do not mean anything.*[5]

there is tremendous outgrowing and undoing. I was deeply moved. It was as if the conditioning of the mind, which had been programmed throughout a millennia of generations, was being undone.

My thoughts do not mean anything.

What a space it provides. How unlimited is the silent mind!

An important thing to learn is to question.
The direct energy of true questioning
will not accept but undo answers.
Intellectual "knowing" is an irresponsibility
if it is not seen as an option.

Each lesson blesses one. How holy is self-knowing. You begin to walk free and pure upon the land full of beauty. As you grow towards your own spaciousness, each lesson continues to undo. Then you realize, with the eyes of wisdom and wonder, the reality of:

My thoughts are images that I have made.[6]

Miracles are swift, happening all the time. But most of us are preoccupied with thought images. Thus, there is not the uncontaminated space between our thoughts for wisdom, virtue, and forgiveness.

These early lessons expand one's horizon, awaken potentials within, and endow the student with the capacity to receive. They represent the beginning of inner awakening. What a transformation!

There is another way of looking at the world.[7]

One begins to have some glimpse of what a miracle is — an instant free of time and personality. With each lesson, as the student moves from miracle to Holy Instant, he realizes that he is not alone.

My holiness envelops everything I see.[8]

God goes with me wherever I go.[9]

The space the lesson imparts makes the Given accessible. To me,

I am determined to see,[10]

means to discover the energy of pure attention that is free of thought.

By the time I got to Lesson 99,

Salvation is my only function here.[11]

and Lesson 100,

My part is essential to God's plan for salvation.[12]

what transpired through me had changed my values and affected my entire thought system. Now I had what I never quite knew before. Honesty, function, and responsibility are synonymous and endow one with the newness of a broad vision and sympathy for mankind. When transformation takes place in man, he is blessed. By this newness, I felt cleansed of all anxiety, insecurity, and projections. A great realization shook me through and through with its power and delight — that the lifestyle of *A Course In Miracles* is intrinsic and free of conflict; because it is non-contradictory, it extends what it is and does not do one thing for the sake of another.

I felt the joy of an eternal gratefulness and declared that the Name of God cannot be commercialized — that I would share *A Course In Miracles*, tuition-free, with anyone who was serious and had the capacity to receive what was not of the illusion of thought and ideas.

HOW CAN THE NAME OF GOD BE COMMERCIALIZED?

No one who extends the Will of God, or who has heard the voice that precedes thought, can ever commercialize the Absolute. The saints and the prophets of God have never bought and sold God for money. Inherent within the God-given function is security, for what such a man does is an extension of the order of the universe.

On Easter, the day of Resurrection, 1983, the involuntary action of clarity within myself initiated the Non-Commercialized Action for the first time in the history of the New World.

Thus began the One Year Non-Commercialized Retreat to bring *A Course In Miracles,* with its curriculum of *Text, Workbook For Students* of three hundred sixty-five lessons, and *Manual for Teachers,* into application. The retreat started with forty-nine people from all over the country who had gathered in Los Angeles where we were situated. There is wisdom in an action that begins within oneself. It is the simplicity of this direct action which discovers: wherever you are is the right place and whatever you have is all you need for an adequate response to greet the action of Life.

The retreat took place in the city rather than in the country, removed from one's daily life. The Course is for people who are active in the world. To first project images of one's own place with its greenery and then raise money for a community or ashram is a violation of the lifestyle of *A Course In Miracles*, and also a contradiction to self-reliance. Heed the words of Henry David Thoreau:

> "Beware of all enterprises
> that require new clothes."[13]

— or new property with raised money.

The participants, having their own energy, came to Los Angeles, grouped together, rented their own places, and signed their leases. No one missed a session, and in less than a week everyone was settled. The lifestyle of *A Course In Miracles* makes every action, every day, meaningful and alive.

We had two sessions daily, and often three or four, sometimes with smaller groups. Years before, it had been intimated to me:

> "Get healthy and strong. You will be needed.
> The path is clear. The way will be shown, and
> there is service."

In preparation, I had spent three years of contemplative life alone in silence. I was then led to do workshops and retreats and even a Forty Days in the Wilderness Retreat with a group of one hundred and twelve people. Here we started each session after one hour of sitting in silence.*

*   *   *

Jesus, Who speaks in the first person in the *Text* of *A Course In Miracles*, states:

I am in charge of the process of Atonement.[14]

("Atonement" means the ending of separation.) Later He assures us:

I will teach with you and live with you
if you will think with me.[15]

But *...if you will think with me* is where the challenge is, for Jesus has no levels. The thoughts He thinks with are Absolute. Unless we undo our relative knowledge of half-truths, we remain untrue to ourselves and are not in communication with Him. Nor do we know the truth of miracles or the Holy Instant.

The Course introduces man to his God-nature.

---

* The years and events which led up to the One Year Non-Commercialized Retreat: A Serious Study of *A Course In Miracles* are documented in Tara Singh's *The Voice That Precedes Thought*, published by Life Action Press in 1987. (Editor)

I am as God created me.[16]

Love, Which created me, is what I am.[17]

Forgiveness offers me everything I want.[18]

To realize the truth of these lessons demands self-honesty. Where there is no conflict of levels, there is the energy of attention. The Law is: attention dispels thought.

There are many sincere people who teach and preach the Gospels and who are leaders of society, but sincerity is not honesty. It is honesty that is free of insecurity. And it is insight that is independent of the unfulfillment and illusions of personality.

What does it mean to be truly objective? When you are objective you give attention, because you are not involved in any kind of bias, or likes and dislikes; you are impersonal. Being truly objective invokes a new and different intelligence. Then you can be responsible for what you say and do.

*   *   *

After the One Year, twenty participants stayed on who were determined to live by the lifestyle of *A Course In Miracles*. The Presence that had never left throughout the Year now intensified. The authenticity of the situation renewed each one and undid many of the options. However, to evolve to self-reliance is as great a challenge as living a life of eternal values and "In God We Trust,"[19] this nation's protection.

"The Statement Of The Participants" depicts the aspiration and atmosphere that surrounded the second year of the Non-Commercialized Retreat.

*   *   *

THE STATEMENT OF THE PARTICIPANTS

As students of *A Course In Miracles,*
we are the disciples of the One in charge of Atonement.
He is to us — Alive.
We think with Him.
Whatever we do, is done by — Him.

Ours is the Ministry of Gratefulness.
Together, productive and self-reliant,
we stand on our own feet
to bring the Course into application in our lives
and prepare to see man, in Truth,
as the Altar of God on Earth.
And extend to the tired world,
taxed by meaningless work,
the message of — Fulfillment.

We have no projects,
no ambition to own a community, or external ashrams;
we do not commercialize life,
nor ask for donations.

Our own sincerity and purity of work
makes our life intrinsic.

We are strengthened by the power of seeing a — Fact,
and the integrity of single purpose.

We do not work for another
and see no man contaminated by external unreality.

We have found our — Calling,
having heard the whisper of Absolute Knowledge.
Gratefulness, Forgiveness, Non-attachment are — Real.
And fulfillment already is a part of — Love.

"IN GOD WE TRUST."

*   *   *

A new order emerged with the need of professionalism in all aspects of the work — transcribing the tapes, indexing, compiling, designing, editing. Each person acted from his own energy in a spirit of cooperation. Thus, the transition from having a job to having one's own work began.

Self-reliance is a difficult undertaking in present society controlled as it is by monetary systems and monopolies of every description. The bare subsistence of twenty men and women, having no place of their own, paying rent, food, and operating expenses, makes self-reliance almost impossible. The monthly rent, housing twenty people in a city, is a colossal amount. The Foundation for Life Action, a federally approved, nonprofit, educational foundation was founded on its own ethics and was determined not to seek donations, nor accept charity. From time to time, large offers of money were refused because they would interfere in the integrity of our experiment.

The transition from having one's own work to having a job has played havoc in human society and has changed man's very mentality, culture, and psyche. Man knows so little of what he has lost; he doesn't know how much poorer and dependent he is upon the political, economic, and other systems that regulate the lives of men all over the world. Time will reveal that one cannot depend on the externals. A society, busy in the midst of the hustle and bustle of its own routine, can also become like a desert without a drop of water to drink.*

No matter how productive you are, you still need capital for equipment — to operate and produce, to promote and sell. How much capital is required for publishing books and manufacturing tapes in a market monopolized by mass-producers!

Thus, "In God We Trust" is the most difficult truth for thought to acknowledge. As a belief, it is a mere cliche. But trust and faith are, in their reality, not abstract ideas. Trust and faith are the direct certainty that knows no insecurity at all. Faith is wordless. Absolute. It has the unstrained face of a child.

We were beginning to discover that security is inherent in the God-given function. At first, one person began to realize this; but Truth is the Given, and what is

---

* For further discussion of these topics, see Tara Singh's *The Future Of Mankind — The Branching Of The Road*, published by the Foundation for Life Action in 1986. (Editor)

given to one is for the whole. It is this that cannot be commercialized. Thus, we continued to share the miracles imparted and all that unfolded. Our relationship with the Course assumed a totally different meaning. We had to find the strength within ourselves to know:

> ...let us receive only what You have given,
> and accept but this into the minds
> which You created and which You love.[20]

It is not easy to truthfully say:

> Father...help us to accept
> our true relationship with You,
> in which there are no illusions,
> and where none can ever enter.[21]

We were inexperienced in the ways of self-reliance, never taking advantage of another, intrinsic work, and having something of our own to give. But we worked with the resources at hand, rather than what we "should" have. To discover our own potential, we had to drop "should be" from our vocabulary. Moving from "what is" to "what should be" is not the thought system of *A Course In Miracles*.

The simplicity and certainty of true productivity, of this too we knew nothing. We had to probe into the deeper meanings of the words we thought we understood.

We found self-reliance and fulfillment to be synonymous. To know no lack is the most difficult challenge for personality to face. Its fear and doubt sabotage everything. What is required not to undermine God's Plan for Salvation?[22]

Nothing is understood in isolation. Once thought has fragmented the whole, misperception follows. But the one amongst us was not afraid of failure because he was not seeking success.

And now, here we are, four and a half years later, with nine books, five thousand tapes, a highly professional presentation, and, as a group,

...determined to see things differently.[23]

*   *   *

The purpose of the Foundation For Life Action is to be with Eternal Laws so that it does not become an organization. The group of twenty, blessed with harmonious and productive life, has undertaken not to be success-oriented, not to expand but to grow, and above all, to adhere to internal awakening. We are a festive, hardworking group, charged by the work we do.

The Foundation for Life Action is a School situated at *The Branching Of The Road*, that represents *A Course In Miracles* in this time of "celestial speed-up."[24]

When you come to the place where the branch in the road is quite apparent, you cannot go ahead. You must go either one way or the other. For now if you go straight ahead, the way you went before you reached the branch, you will go nowhere. The whole

purpose of coming this far was to decide which branch you will take now. The way you came no longer matters. It can no longer serve.[25]

He thought he learned willingness, but now he sees that he does not know what the willingness is for. And now he must attain a state that may remain impossible to reach for a long, long time.[26]

The energetic action of *A Course In Miracles* upon these planes makes the Absolute Knowledge of God accessible to the individual. The School at *The Branching Of The Road* — "Having The Ears To Hear"[27] — is an extension of the Divine action of *A Course In Miracles*. It is for those who are already students, who are emptied of self and come NOT TO LEARN, BUT TO *BE*,[28] and who have "the ears to hear."

The primary function of the School is to train teachers to bring *A Course In Miracles* into application. It deals with the inherent unwillingness in the individual to change, and insists upon direct contact with the Holy Spirit to undo and to bring the Course into application, and to come to the energy of First Thought, free of conflict. It exists for the serious few, the incorruptible, who cannot live without the True Knowledge of God.

To learn this Course requires willingness to question every value that you hold. Not one can be kept hidden and obscure but it will jeopardize your learning.[29]

Unwillingness, we have discovered, is one of the strongest ...*blocks to the awareness of love's presence.*[30] Mere enthusiasm is not enough. There is an underlying resistance within man to change and live by the indivisible law of love. The School at *The Branching Of The Road* is a place where resistance to correction, unwillingness, a sense of lack, and irresponsibility are to be undone.

*   *   *

A Course In Miracles is very challenging. Its teacher, too, is a challenging person and will not let the student accept mere ideas as Truth, nor concepts and dogma as actual facts. The teacher is the one who has outgrown success in order to share the miracles of the Course. But it takes discrimination to recognize a fact.

It is a fact that imparts the energy that undoes misperceptions instantly and purifies the mind. A fact is a gift of insight, independent of thought. Our "knowings" have become our bondage. We deceive ourselves so willingly. Faced with a fact that transcends duality, there is not much anyone has to say. We have seen that to say, "I understand," means nothing — that verbal understanding has no validity whatsoever. It is Truth that relates one to the whole, not the verbal. Humility, and not the vanity of "knowing," is religious. Religion is a State of Being, not a belief.

*   *   *

Jesus said:

"I CAN OF MINE OWN SELF DO NOTHING."[31]

He spent three years with His apostles, and it has taken us four and a half years to discover that the ego makes sure never to find what it seeks.[32] Yet there are group leaders of *A Course In Miracles* everywhere selling miracles and holy instants as if they were conducting a yard sale. The fact of the matter is: very few people are serious. To most of us, learning — the brain activity — is still captivating, for it gives the illusion of self-improvement.

But undoing is the basic premise of the Course. It is in the undoing of illusions or beliefs that miracles take place. The Holy Spirit knows the perfection of the Son of God and assists the student to come to the awareness of:

I am as God created me.[33]

The sharing of truth requires a totally different thought system than the one to which we presently adhere. An education that awakens the vast potentials of man's higher faculties demands the intimacy of one-to-one relationship. It is essential. In that deep communication, "where two or more gather,"[34] is the grace of God. The books, *Commentaries On A Course In Miracles*, as well as *Dialogues On A Course In Miracles*, evolved out of group discussions during the four years of the retreat.

I am among the ministers of God,
And I am grateful that I have the means
By which to recognize that I am free.

The world recedes as we light up our minds, and realize these holy words are true. They are the message sent to us today from our Creator. Now we demonstrate how they have changed our minds about ourselves, and what our function is.[35]

This is our direction in what *A Course In Miracles* calls the *...journey without distance.*[36]

The energy of first thought brings order in life that continues to serve mankind forever. The work of the Foundation for Life Action is to bring that kind of an order into the lives of people. Goodness and love can take no sides or think in terms of advantage. Self-reliance, intrinsic work, and having something of one's own to give purify a man and introduce him to his own Self.

The wise does not abide by concepts
the world adheres to;
having given himself the gift of self-honesty,
his life is a service to humanity for all time.
Only those who have attachments suffer.
One who lives by Truth
has no desires at all.

Each one of us has the potential
to be free from the pressure of alternatives
now that the Given,
the True Knowledge of *A Course In Miracles*,
is made directly accessible to the individual.

Tara Singh
August, 1987

*   *   *

The previous edition of *How To Learn From A Course In Miracles* originated from sharings from the One Year Non-Commercialized Retreat.

This expanded, second edition contains new material shared during the additional four years and represents the seriousness of the interactions with the students of the Retreat.

*   *   *

FOREWORD

As I EMERGED FROM a three year period in silent retreat, I was introduced to *A Course In Miracles* for the first time. For me, it was the meeting of the Spirit of *A Course In Miracles*. I recognized instantly that it was the Thoughts of God.

This contact with *A Course In Miracles* completed something in me. I knew my function the minute I read:

Nothing real can be threatened.
Nothing unreal exists.[1]

What took place in that instant has never left me. It is a bond with another Reality, the impeccability of which inspires one.

I had often wondered why, out of all the scriptures of the world, there was not a single step-by-step approach that a person could pursue unto application. I was very impressed by Moses parting the sea, and the wondrous things the other God-lit men and prophets had done, but it did not alter anything in me. It was not my light.

I rejoice that *A Course In Miracles* has its own day-by-day curriculum, as one is held by the hand and led to one's own eternal purity and holiness.

A Course In Miracles invokes the inherent memory of God that initiates an awakening within. It is for the active man living in the world and requires little time for its application. It has emerged out of the New World to bring mankind to new consciousness.

The Course is an action. It does not condemn or judge anyone. It does not react to religions. It deals with the student who reads it, and takes away the idea of dependence and of following another. It brings the student to the discovery of potentials within himself that will enable him to impart something of eternal value.

Once you have the eternal to give, insecurity no longer arises and conflict ends. The question lies in changing. And to change — to be transformed — requires integrity and self-honesty. I have known two God-lit beings, and both have emphasized, "People seldom ever change."

The lessons of *A Course In Miracles* have to be brought into application. Nothing will work unless the truth of the Course is lived. Everything depends on the individual and his integrity.

To discover one's own God-given function is the great gift of Life. What is natural is effortless. The struggle lies in removing the distorted perception of who we assume we are. Being free from his own beliefs is what man calls difficult.

Man's function is to bring the Kingdom of God to earth. He is the bearer of Grace and his holiness is a blessing upon all that is.

Tara Singh

INTRODUCTION

WHAT CAN I SAY about this book
that endeavors to represent the spirit of
A Course In Miracles?

The very benediction the Course imparts
silences me.
It is an action of the Grace of God.
Unhurried, read it lovingly.
The moment you are relaxed,
wisdom will surround you
and the Given becomes accessible.

A Course In Miracles is a joyous adventure.
Each lesson imparts its blessing all day long.
It awakens you to gratefulness
and to your God-given function.

Be still and listen to the truth.

Into Christ's Presence will we enter now,
serenely unaware of everything
except His shining face and perfect Love.
The vision of His face will stay with you,
but there will be an instant
which transcends all vision,
even this, the holiest.
This you will never teach,
for you attained it not through learning.
Yet the vision speaks of your rememberance
of what you knew that instant,
and will surely know again.[1]

PART ONE

1

HOW TO LEARN FROM
A COURSE IN MIRACLES

A COURSE IN MIRACLES is a systematic, divine order of education that reveals our innate perfection. It consists of three volumes: *Text, Workbook For Students,* and *Manual For Teachers.** There are three hundred sixty-five lessons, one for each day of the year.

Reading the Course invokes within you energies that you may never have been sensitive to before. All your questions can get answered. Its purpose is to provide self-sufficiency and eliminate the false premise of

---

* The *Text*, 622 pages, sets forth the concepts on which the thought system of the Course is based. The *Workbook For Students*, 478 pages, is designed to make possible the application of the concepts presented in the *Text*. The *Manual For Teachers*, 88 pages, provides answers to some of the basic questions a student of the Course might ask and defines many of the terms used in the *Text*. (Editor)

helplessness. Therefore, it is to be lived and not just to be read.

> *Do you not see that all your misery comes from the strange belief that you are powerless?*[1]

We cannot apply *A Course In Miracles* as long as we are satisfied with ideas, because the Course is not an idea. It is not abstract. It does not talk *about* something. It speaks from the actuality of Truth Itself.

If you have seen the limitations and the falseness of ideas, then you come to stillness, and you communicate with something beyond your own thought. This is the purpose of the Course, to bring ideas that cannot know Love or Truth to an end. Can we read it this way?

It is reverence that gives us the space to receive that which is not of thought, but of Grace. Reverence frees us from thought and brings the mind to stillness. It activates the heart. When you love something there is the reverence, for it becomes total and whole and has its own atmosphere. Therefore, it is important to learn to read with reverence and space.

A Course In Miracles comes to us at a time when mankind needs a scripture that teaches application. All scriptures are vertical words. Scripture is only scripture when it is not born of separation from God. The purpose of scripture is to end man's limitation and bring him to the wholeness that he is.

Learning, according to *A Course In Miracles*, is the miracle that undoes the belief system of separation. Thus, the basic issue we face is the separation in us that promotes fear, loneliness, and insecurity; and then, in turn, the wishes and "wantings" of unfulfillment.

Miracles offer us the clarity of inner awakening that is the direct experience of,

> *Nothing real can be threatened.*
> *Nothing unreal exists.*[2]

The miracle of the Holy Instant would bring you to objectivity and reveal this fact. It is a different kind of learning.

The ability to see the false as the false is to be free of the false. That moment of freedom is religious. It is the space where the miracle takes place. But if you do not put your whole attention to it, then you are stuck with an idea and not a miracle.

Man's thought system promotes the separation, no matter how sensitive and wise and good its ideas seem. Miracles undo it.

A miracle frees us from the past and future.

Clarity frees us from desires, suffering, and anxiety — for these are self-made, in ignorance of Reality.

Reality is the Will of God, the light of perfection. It is the Divine Decision. The wise, having seen the fallacy of personal decision, makes but one decision: to never make a decision independent of the Will of God.

In our unawareness we make decisions out of loneliness and uncertainty. But there are no uncertainties in Life, nor confusion where there is Love. Only desires, ambitions, and want of activity lead to personal decisions. If we are grateful and at peace, then we discover all needs are already blessed and met.

REALITY IS THE ONLY DECISION.

Knowing this, we would not be slave to our misery that projects wishes and "wantings." If we read with a still mind, we know with certainty God takes perfect care of us. This realized, there is no need for anxiety or worry. This is the Peace of God.

Man is meant to be at peace and in harmony with Life, for AS IS is perfection. But the question is, do we really KNOW this? Are we at peace or are we children of insecurity?

We are talking about *A Course In Miracles* and how to learn from it directly.

Every day we read a lesson from the *Workbook*. For example,

Love created me like Itself.[3]

We may think we know what the word "love" means, but do we? Honesty is required to know the truth of it.

As long as we are content with just words — and most of us are — we will never get to know what it really means. Why is it we have not questioned a word we use so frequently, to discover what is the actual state of Love?

Love, which is of Heaven, is the only state of being that is not pressured by time or anything external. Every single knowing is external to it. Every single word, including the word "love," is external to the actual state of Love. It is uncontaminated by words, and it renews itself every moment. Each of us is of the authenticity of Love.

Every second the planets rotate. What energy! Can you conceive of how many billions upon billions of breaths are taken every second? And all that breathes grows. Can you see the energy behind Life? That energy is what Love is; and the whole of creation is an extension of it. Its first impact dissolves all words, and brings one to innocence, to the purity of a saint. The state of being that knows the Real has the right to use the word "Love." Nothing else has.

The action of the Course is that of Love. It does not influence because it is an action of the awakening of Love, which is independent, and must therefore provide freedom and liberation. It restores your identity with your reality and eternity.

As long as we are going to keep using words without knowing the reality behind the words, we will not know what *A Course In Miracles* imparts. We need to give it space and read it with a quiet mind that is not pressured. Offer your stillness and it will be filled with peace.

How we approach learning from *A Course In Miracles* and the quality of honesty we give it, is all important. We do not want to turn its teachings into another belief within the limited thought system of man, for *A Course In Miracles* is the Thoughts of God and awakens one out of thought to one's own boundlessness.

The *Workbook For Students* begins with the lesson,

> *Nothing I see in this room [on this street, from this window, in this place] means anything.*

It goes on to say,

> *Now look slowly around you.*[4]

Have we paid any heed to the word "slowly"? Have we ever done so? Probably not. It is not all that easy to slow down the thought process. It is like saying "relax." Does your pulse come down instantly because you have used the word "relax"? But if you are in a reverent atmosphere, where you love what you are going to be reading or doing, you are already prepared. You have already stepped out of the momentum of tension and activity, and found a few moments just to BE. The action of relaxation is that it widens the gaps between the thoughts.

Then, when you read, *Now look slowly around you*, you have given yourself the freedom and space to do so.

There are constant reminders in the lessons of the Course that stress "unhurriedly," "slowly." These must be essential because the very first line of the first lesson states:

> *Now look slowly around you, and practice applying*
> *this idea very specifically to whatever you see:*
>
> > *This table does not mean anything.*
> > *This chair does not mean anything.*[5]

The Course insists that you are not to make the practice ritualistic. Ritual means repetition of something. Just saying the words of the lesson does not mean anything.

Could you really look at the hand before you and say,

> *This hand does not mean anything?*

The Course begins with the undoing of our belief systems and our "knowings" — the bondage in which we are caught. It is our conclusions that are being questioned, and the question has the vitality not to accept any of our own verbal answers.

Undoing is essential because we are so highly conditioned. What we think we know is seldom real, for it is only our opinion. We stop short, conclude, and therefore, we never see the whole, the total.

Separated as we are, we tend to separate everything. Anything that is in isolation, to which we give a name, is unreal because everything is part of the whole. And unless we see the whole, we are not seeing at all.

Each lesson of the Course brings our separation to our awareness, and in an instant, an awakening to end that separation. For to know the truth is to bring it to application instantly.

> *The truth is true. Nothing else matters, nothing else is real, and everything beside it is not there. Let Me make the one distinction for you that you cannot make, but need to learn. Your faith in nothing is deceiving you. Offer your faith to Me, and I will place it gently in the holy place where it belongs. You will find no deception there, but only the simple truth. And you will love it because you will understand it.*[6]

Within that moment you can behold eternity. Therefore, you are free from time, and you discover your own reality, your boundlessness, its sacred moment. That is the moment in which the miracle has taken place. The miracle is when time ceases and eternity is.

The Course has much more to give than intellectual knowledge. It is to end the separation in one's life and bring one to the wholeness of one's being. One is cleansed with the purity of one's own Reality!

> *I am not a body. I am free.*
> *For I am still as God created me.*[7]

Where there is the body, there is thought. They are not two phenomena. If one came to the truth of *I am not a body*, then one would say, *I am free.* Each individual would realize, *I am still as God created me.* Concepts of punishment, karma, and guilt come to an end.

A Course In Miracles is based on each person's inherent perfection and our approach to reading it should be based on our perfection as well.

If the god we seek is a god born out of our unfulfillment, he will end up being a projection of our unfulfillment. A projection is an image, not the Truth. The Course says,

God is with me. I live and move in Him.[8]

True relationship exists at the eternal level. The river is related to the ocean, to the sky. Everything is related. Nothing can exist by itself. Relationship is that you are related to the planets, to the light, to the earth, to everything. You could not exist without them for nothing can exist in isolation. In relationship, there is no such thing as fear, insecurity, or unfulfillment.

The flower is a flower, and it is not unfulfilled. It is the joy of its own perfection. A flower has no wishes. It does not want to be a chair or a pot. If you could see the flower, it could bring you to stillness. Your distractions and wishings and "wantings" would end also. For in that moment you are related to wholeness.

Look at the star and it introduces you to your own eternity. Light years away, but you can relate with it. If you have truly seen it, it silences your mind. If you are preoccupied while looking at it, you merely look but do not see.

The Course tells us,

> *Miracles are seen in light.*[9]

This is not the physical light of the sun. The sun is a small affair. There are other spheres that are not lit with this little sun. This is a Light that has a million suns in it. It is the Light in which there is understanding. It is not an understanding *of* something; because then, that thing is there, and you are here. Do you see the separation so-called understanding creates? To the Light of awareness, nothing is outside of you. We are talking about a state where appearances disappear and One Reality is.

Unfortunately, we have, over the centuries, become obsessed with the accumulation of more and more knowledge. This mania of moreness keeps unfulfillment alive and is what regulates our intellectual faculties. Can we approach learning from a new premise: fulfillment?

We are talking about learning with an intent to be free of preoccupation, and not to accumulate information. Thus, we read differently.

Jesus continually repeats in the Bible,

> "HE THAT HATH EARS TO HEAR, LET HIM HEAR."[10]

Will you listen? We usually do not listen because we interpret what we hear and read with our own thoughts.

We are listening to our interpretations, are we not? We assess the other person: "I like this." "I do not like that." And the chatter goes on.

The minute we are really attentive, thoughts cease. For example, we are attentive if we run into a rattlesnake. We do not interpret whether it is male or female.

We are capable of coming to attention. But as long as we are lukewarm, we are not going to do so. We fall back into thought that says, "I am going to do it tomorrow." Thought lives by postponement.

We never see that postponement is a thought process, and it is not real. It is still ideas. It will crumble away because ideas, like emotions, subside, rise and fall. There is no consistency in them.

But there is consistency when we are totally attentive, because in that moment, we are free from brain activity. There is space to be part of the Mind of God that we are.

We will know the Mind of God when the chatter of the brain is silenced. The brain has its senses; it is used for survival; it collects memories. But the mind is the Mind of God of which we are all a part.

When the brain does not interfere, stillness introduces us to the Mind of God. We discover that every single being is blessed, being part of the Mind of God. And there is no longer any separation between you and me. At the brain level, there is separation. At the Mind level, we are all One.

It is the Mind of God that is religious, not the brain. The brain can be Hindu, Moslem, or Christian. It is conditioned, shaped by the environment, by personal experience. But the Mind of God is neither conditioned nor subject to experience.

Once that fact is established, our relationship with *A Course In Miracles* undergoes a change. We become more attentive and read it differently. We can read a lesson in the Course, which would be using words to begin with, but every sentence would lead us from our thought to the Mind of God.

This is the unique thing about the Course. Organized religions tell us what Jesus did, what Mohammed did, and what Lord Rama did. *A Course In Miracles* does not tell us what somebody else did. It does not preach. It brings us to stillness and to the Mind of God. This all depends, however, on how serious and with what quality of reverence we read it. If liberation is our interest, then we value there is something that has, inherent in it, a blessing to take us out of our thought process — our brain preoccupation — to a different state.

While we read, there is the questioning of our unrealized words and the discovery of our attachment to our thoughts — thus, an awakening to the newness beyond the words. This actuality of direct experience takes place in the reading of the Course if there is the attention.

My mind is preoccupied with past thoughts.[11]

This is the problem. We cannot harness the energy of the Present. We are not alive to the moment, to receive or radiate the creative energy of the Present that this planet needs. Man's function is to bring the Kingdom of God to earth. And most of us are lost in the past.

Lesson after lesson, the Course begins with questioning and undoing to free us from the past. It goes on to say,

> *I see nothing as it is now.*[12]

What a simple way of saying it. The Course really is a course in miracles so that you come to truth, to wholeness, and to rightmindedness. It is in rightmindedness that miracles take place.

To say this sincerely,

> *My thoughts do not mean anything,*[13]

is to save a lifetime. This is the tenth lesson. Is there anything in the world that can bring a person to this state and the innocence of humility within ten days?

As we read, we begin to value what the Course is, and the reverence and love for it increase. The lesson continues:

> *This idea applies to all the thoughts of which you are aware, or become aware in the practice periods. The reason the idea is applicable to all of them is that they are not your real thoughts.*[14]

There are real thoughts of which we are not aware. This is quite a discovery!

> We have made this distinction before, and will do so again. You have no basis for comparison as yet. When you do, you will have no doubt that what you once believed were your thoughts did not mean anything.[15]

What an awakening! It is like the Lord holding us by the hand, and in ten simple days, bringing a total transformation.

There is a great deal of joy and excitement in the Course. It brings one to passion. The interest is there, and we are getting closer to the Present and our own holiness. We are becoming our real Self.

The outgrowing is taking place. The newness is rearing its head. We are beginning to question our own fanaticism, the beliefs that we knew. Now we are willing to see — to die to the past and to conditioning. We are no longer subject to the past, and a rebirth takes place.

Then the significant eleventh lesson:

> My meaningless thoughts
> are showing me a meaningless world.[16]

To just see and serve the meaningless world and to die is to never have lived.

The Course continues,

A meaningless world engenders fear.[17]

There is fear because our values are meaningless. One country holds one value, and another country holds another value. Because they are different, they clash; and both are meaningless.

But,

God did not create a meaningless world.[18]

We see that there are two worlds: the God-created world, without which nothing would exist, and the manmade world of the meaningless. As we begin to free ourselves from the manmade world, we see that the God-created world is the sustainer. Man did not create the air we breathe, nor the water we drink, nor the night sky, nor the food we eat.

How we have cut ourselves off from the God-created world through anxieties and worries! So many of us spend our lives and God-given energy supporting the meaningless.

My thoughts are images that I have made.

It is because the thoughts you think you think appear as images that you do not recognize them as nothing.[19]

See that they are but your images.

You think you think them, and so you think you see them. This is how your "seeing" was made. This is

> the function you have given your body's eyes. It is
> not seeing. It is image-making. It takes the place of
> seeing, replacing vision with illusions.[20]

The Course goes on to say,

> These exercises will not reveal knowledge to you.
> But they will prepare the way to it.[21]

The reader begins to see how he is caught in his own images. Vision is our natural state, and we have replaced it with the illusions of images. And the lesson comfortingly says that our images will be replaced. Inherent in every lesson, in every line, is the blessing to bring one to the clarity of truth.

It is the Will of God, His Power, His Blessing, that the goal of the Course be accomplished within one year by anyone who studies it with integrity and devotion. Please realize what this statement means. What else could you ever want?

If there is the potential in any one lesson to bring you to wholeness, how will you approach it? Will you try to fit it into your scheme of life, your schedule? If so, you are not ready to fit into God's Mind. Are you willing to kindly observe this?

Are you reading *A Course In Miracles* as an idea, to improve yourself? The minute you reduce it to ideas, it is no different than anything else, and you have not received the miracle it has to offer. Why do we reduce it to ideas? Have we ever done anything else, whether it be the Bible, the Koran, or the Vedas? And what "I am" continues. Nothing interrupts the old. Somewhere we have to see that we have to outgrow the self.

We are talking about the approach because much depends on how we read. I have seldom met anyone who knows how to read. We read the words, but the words are not the thing. Our words have meaning at the level of unreality — things we have projected. Yet to dissolve thought takes a different kind of reading, a different quality of attention.

> *Forget not that the motivation for this course is the attainment and the keeping of the state of peace. Given this state the mind is quiet, and the condition in which God is remembered is attained....*
>
> *To learn this course requires willingness to question every value that you hold. Not one can be kept hidden and obscure but it will jeopardize your learning. No belief is neutral.*[22]

Are you approaching *A Course In Miracles* because you really want to step out of the constant preoccupation that gives you no rest? Do you want to bring the deceptions of the brain to silence? If there is that burning need, then your relationship with the Course becomes different.

Yet people have read it over and over without realizing the truth of it. Can you read it with the intensity of interest that will bring you to the State? It requires that you place a challenge before yourself. For without seriousness, the reading becomes ritual. The brain loves habit; it functions in terms of routine.

Each sentence in the Course confronts us with a challenge. Can we give it the inner space to unfold? Usually when a challenge comes, we put it off. We do not recognize the cause of the inadequacy that cannot respond to the challenge at the moment.

Where does the energy go? How do we dissipate it? It is this questioning and awareness that brings about a change in lifestyle. In this urgency of response there is no gap, no time to acknowledge inadequacy. For helplessness is our belief. It is not a reality.

The action of helplessness is compromise. Are you willing to put compromises away instantly as you read? This is application. This is discovery.

We have to realize the importance of intent. Then there is urgency. Urgency brings one to attention. The vitality of urgency alone can deal with the nonchalant attitude of compromise, and in so doing, come to passion.

A transformation takes place. One becomes the co-creator. Do you read the Course as a co-creator, so that by the time you have finished, you have ended the compromise and you are totally present? It is such a different way of reading.

Whatever questions the manmade thought system is already the action of God's Grace. Right away the Course imparts to you a new willingness to see.

I am responsible for what I see.
I choose the feelings I experience,
and I decide upon the goal I would achieve.
And everything that seems to happen to me
I ask for, and receive as I have asked.[23]

A Course In Miracles is a joyous adventure. It is not to be made into a habit. The daily lesson carries its blessing all day long. It becomes an effortless action, and a great joy.

My present happiness is all I see.[24]

You need never be touched by the fear of insecurity, for it is largely psychological. Thus, you begin to extend the peace of God on earth,

"THY WILL BE DONE IN EARTH,
AS IT IS IN HEAVEN."[25]

And this is where you hold hands, as offered in,

If it helps you,
think of me holding your hand and leading you.
And I assure you
this will be no idle fantasy.[26]

What a benediction to know you have never been alone! Light and Love, the Given, have always surrounded you. To realize that the Given is accessible is the strength.

What a gift of God to each one who has *A Course In Miracles*!

The Course helps us with the application of the truth imparted. Yet we know this intellectually, like we know that we should not lie, or we should love our neighbor. But we do not know how to bring it into application. The knowing of ideas does not mean much.

The idea is abstract because it is based on duality. The Course does not go into duality. It dissolves the duality even between you and God. It says your will is one with God's. And God's Will is your will.

Gradually, we are getting used to the One rather than to fragmentation and separation. What a miracle! You would think one would leap with joy for discovering one is and can be liberated.

The Course states we have become conditioned and are caught in habit and error. It points out that these can be corrected.

Truth will correct all errors in my mind.[27]

Correction is your function. Having met your function, you become an extension of the Course. And because errors can be corrected, you cannot be indifferent to your own or anyone else's. When your function becomes:

Salvation is my only function here,[28]

conflict ends and you realize:

I will accept my part in God's plan for salvation.[29]

By now, you must learn to extend what you have realized as the truth. When you begin to extend, then you become the bearer of Light. Thus the Course brings you to your function.

For what God gives can only be good.[30]

Can you trust in that?

*And I accept but what He gives
as what belongs to me.*[31]

Look at the honor God gives His Children. Having given us all creation, He then says, "You are not even under my obligation. This belongs to you." We are given freedom from the very beginning. What sacredness is the glory of God, our Father! There is nothing for us to want or be distracted by.

The *Workbook For Students* states,

All things are lessons God would have me learn.

*A lesson is a miracle which God offers to me,
in place of thoughts I made that hurt me.*[32]

No matter what they are and how good they may seem, all the thoughts we make invariably hurt us.

*What I learn of Him
becomes the way I am set free.*[33]

What I learn from Him is the miracle, being a moment of clarity in which time ceases. What I learn of Him frees me from my own limited decisions.

> *And so I choose to learn His lessons*
> *and forget my own.*[34]

Can you forget your own? We are under the pressure of our needs, our tomorrows, our yesterdays, and the whole personality issue. At the miracle level, however, there are no personalities. You are in the present, and nothing else is real.

The Course shares,

> *I place the future in the Hands of God.*[35]

What a carefree contentment!

It also says,

> *The past is gone; the future is not yet.*
> *Now am I freed from both.*[36]

How spacious is the eternal *now*. The Course is immediate. Can you feel instantly that you are freed from past and future? Will you no longer dwell on the past? The future is not yet, and so you need not worry about that.

If you are just going to read it, and not touch upon the state, then know you are depriving yourself. For as long as there is past and future, there can be no peace. Where past and future no longer exist, there neither is a body.

Thought itself disappears. If the thought remains, then you have not read it.

I am sustained by the Love of God.[37]

You do not even have to seek it. You merely have to realize that Love is what you came to give. The choice is yours, having free will.

Father, it is today that I am free,
because my will is Yours.[38]

The choice is either peace, or thought of past and future, peopled with the personalities of unreality. You want the Peace of God, but it cannot be without letting go of the illusion of past and future ordeals.

An unlived Truth remains untrue. To know the Truth is to bring it to application instantly. In the absence of application, life remains personal.

To the Christ State, body and thoughts are external, for they are of the world of separation. Thought only came into being after separation took place, whereas salvation is the release from thoughts that hurt us.

The language of the co-creator is non-personal, thus different.

Is it a loss to find a world instead where losing is
impossible; where love endures forever, hate cannot
exist and vengeance has no meaning? Is it loss to
find all things you really want, and know they have
no ending and they will remain exactly as you want

them throughout time? Yet even they will be exchanged at last for what we cannot speak of, for you go from there to where words fail entirely, into a silence where the language is unspoken and yet surely understood.

Communication, unambiguous and plain as day, remains unlimited for all eternity. And God Himself speaks to His Son, as His Son speaks to Him. Their language has no words, for what They say cannot be symbolized. Their knowledge is direct and wholly shared and wholly one. How far away from this are you who stay bound to this world. And yet how near are you, when you exchange it for the world you want.

Now is the last step certain; now you stand an instant's space away from timelessness.[39]

The words of *A Course In Miracles* inspire you to the state of stillness. The Course carries its eternal peace and awakens the Light in you.

When you have read three-fourths of the *Text* and the *Workbook*, then it says: You have come a long way, and now you cannot go back. Is that not beautiful? Something has happened to fundamentally change your life. Is that not a benediction?

The introduction of reason into the ego's thought system is the beginning of its undoing, for reason and the ego are contradictory. Nor is it possible for them to coexist in your awareness. For reason's goal is to make plain, and therefore obvious. You can see reason....[40]

When you come to the place where the branch in the road is quite apparent, you cannot go ahead. You must go either one way or the other....No one who reaches this far can make the wrong decision, although he can delay. And there is no part of the journey that seems more hopeless and futile than standing where the road branches, and not deciding on which way to go.

It is but the first few steps along the right way that seem hard, for you have chosen, although you still may think you can go back and make the other choice. This is not so. A choice made with the power of Heaven to uphold it cannot be undone. Your way is decided. There will be nothing you will not be told, if you acknowledge this.[41]

You have one more step to take. The Course says you have the choice of going ahead, but you do not have the choice of going back.

Then it states,

This course is easy just because it makes no compromise. Yet it seems difficult to those who still believe that compromise is possible.[42]

If you took the step, you would sense a new blessing, a charge of vitality, a vivid sense of His Presence.

> *You have come far along the way of truth; too far to falter now. Just one step more, and every vestige of the fear of God will melt away in love.*[43]

The only response you have is to realize you and your brother are the extension of One Life. You no longer look upon what he does in a body, but see his holiness.

> *You would oppose this course because it teaches you you are alike. You have no purpose that is not the same, and none your Father does not share with you. For your relationship has been made clean of special goals. And would you now defeat the goal of holiness that Heaven gave it?*[44]

> *Choose, then, his body or his holiness as what you want to see, and which you choose is yours to look upon. Yet will you choose in countless situations, and through time that seems to have no end, until the truth be your decision. For eternity is not regained by still one more denial of Christ in him. And where is your salvation, if he is but a body? Where is your peace but in his holiness? And where is God Himself but in that part of Him He set forever in your brother's holiness, that you might see the truth about yourself, set forth at last in terms you recognized and understood?*

> *Your brother's holiness is sacrament and benediction unto you. His errors cannot withhold God's blessing from himself, nor you who see him truly. His mistakes can cause delay, which it is given you to take from him, that both may end a journey that*

has never begun, and needs no end. What never was
is not a part of you. Yet you will think it is, until
you realize that it is not a part of him who stands
beside you. He is the mirror of yourself, wherein you
see the judgment you have laid on both of you. The
Christ in you beholds his holiness.[45]

This is the ending of the world — the illusion of appearance. Here one realizes the truth and value of,

"LOVE YE ONE ANOTHER."[46]

And there is peace upon the earth.

Wherever there is such an awakened being, there is a radiance, a peace. Even the birds and the animals are not afraid, for it takes all the hysteria and the tensions out of the air.

And when such a being walks through the woods or through the city, he leaves that peace there. Everything becomes consecrated and blessed, for that being remains untouched by words.

Please do not underestimate yourself.

You carry a blessing with you.

Be at peace,
and know you are part of Eternity.

> *The certain are perfectly calm,*
> *because they are not in doubt.*

They do not raise questions,
because nothing questionable enters their minds.
This holds them in perfect serenity,
because this is what they share,
knowing what they are.[47]

PART TWO

2

THE FIRST FORTY LESSONS

How PRECIOUS IS SILENCE. It is complete. In stillness the brain renews itself and every cell in the body is affected. The stillness becomes so intensified you are not even aware you are a body. There is no greater healing than to be of a silent mind.

In stillness there is no duality, but an awareness that just observes. It is very intelligent. Problems and opinions — the false — are dissolved. The still mind is aware of the arrival and disappearance of sounds externally, but they do not disturb the stillness because there is no opinion about them. The goodness of a still mind absorbs everything and blesses it.

When silence, or stillness, enters one's life, it makes you aware of all that is unessential, all that is born of

ideas. And it starts to undo. It begins to outgrow —
beliefs, concepts, psychological hurts — like a child
outgrows toys and dolls.

What else do you think the silence discovers? It begins
to discover:

> *Nothing I see... means anything.*[1]

> *I have given everything I see...*
> *all the meaning that it has for me.*[2]

See the truth of it, not just the words. It becomes simple
and direct. *Nothing I see means anything.* When you see the
truth of this, it brings the mind to stillness, to relaxation.
That's what energizes an awakening within us. Don't
activate other thoughts. Let it be a discovery, a
benediction. *I have given everything I see all the meaning that
it has for me!* Don't try to free yourself from it; you'll only
start acting through thought to do so. Just seeing the truth
of it is enough.

Seeing is an action; "trying" is not an action but a
reaction. Action eliminates; that which "tries" is effort
and makes life personal. One is the given; the other is a
striving.

Wisdom lies in being relaxed and present with the
lesson. You haven't read it if you are still caught in your
"knowings" and accumulation of knowledge. If you are
still giving meaning to your activities, you've not read it.
If you have not established a relationship with the

process of Atonement,[3] you are lost in your own doing, preoccupied with your own survival.

> *I have given everything I see...*
> *all the meaning that it has for me.*

These lessons have much deeper significance than we realize; so please do them with a quality of reverence. This is essential because without reverence we cannot receive. Everything man needs to know is found in *A Course In Miracles.* How much gratefulness is due it! All the wealth in the world could not buy what the Course does to a person.

Each one of us has the potential to know the Course. What do I mean by "potential"? Potential means that we have the capacity to receive that which is of God. Without the potential, we could not receive it.

When are we with the potential? We *are* the potential — and yet we are not aware of it. Religions and gurus have tried to preoccupy us with doing things: mantras, yoga, all kinds of techniques, and so forth. But the person who knows what potential is has outgrown everything; he has discovered that "me and mine" is abstract, that it's not real. He sees, "As a potential, I am freed from my own personality!" The potential, then, outgrows selfhood.

The first action of the potential is that it silences the brain. We have the potential to silence ourselves totally. Once we are silenced, there is no tomorrow and no yesterday.

The potential has the capacity of being very attentive. It is in this attention that the mind comes to stillness. The attentiveness dissolves all words, all "wantings." It is a state of fulfillment. The stillness, then, begins to impart its truth to you:

I do not understand anything I see.[4]

You begin to question, "How do I see? Is this true that I do not understand anything I see?" How would potential see it? It would see it with a still mind. See if you can come to that still mind. Just drop everything for a moment. Then whatever you look at, you are not dividing anymore; it's a still mind looking at things without fragmenting them, without naming them. The minute we start naming a thing, we are giving it meaning.

See how the process of fragmentation has taken place within us. This tendency to make distinctions is what separates. And we call that "knowing." Separation is what we call "knowing." The more we become caught in fragmentation — the separation that divides things — the more it prevents the understanding of what is eternal. The only real "knowing" is the direct experience in which the separation has ended in you.

I do not understand anything — not even what a flower is. Do we understand what it is other than the name we have given it? Could you separate the flower from the soil? Could you separate it from the sun, the seasons? Where would it end? The flower extends everything in creation. It cannot be isolated. When you understand it that way, you have also ended your isolation, your separation.

What would have to take place in order not to make distinctions? You would have to observe with a still mind, wouldn't you? When the mind is still, there is no judgment.

Try to look around with that still mind, without naming anything — just out of serenity, without any opinion, without any judgment. When you're still, this is what happens.

Then you discover:

These thoughts do not mean anything.[5]

Can you truthfully say that? What does thought give importance to? Is it not to one's own attachments? We know very little other than the personal, circumscribed, limited world of "me and mine." *These thoughts do not mean anything* because they are personal.

And what is thought? All thought is reaction and therefore, meaningless. Thought is opinion, it's personal; and therefore, it limits one. If you discovered this all day long — about your own thought — what would happen?

You wouldn't fit into the world. And what a good thing that would be! There would be no fear — of losing your job or anything else. Everything would become secondary. You would have a function that takes care of everything. You have become a law unto yourself and you bless all of creation. You are no longer subordinated to the gross.

The difficulty comes when you say, "I believe that now, but I've got to make a living. I can't apply it." This belief that we cannot bring truth to application is to be questioned. Would you be daring enough to question this belief?

There is a challenge that thought always evades — the challenge of action. Action has the power and vitality to dissolve thought. It purifies us and cleanses us of the thoughts that are meaningless. If we could give ourselves the gift of silence, we would know what action is.

Do you feel the challenge this poses? We have to cope with our feelings of inadequacy in dealing with the challenge. What do we do with our sense of inadequacy? Ignore it? Get depressed by it? That's as good an escape as anything else. But time isn't going to make it any easier. Postponing is no solution and yet we can't seem to prevent the postponing: "I hope I can do it tomorrow."

So, our inadequacies have invented a tomorrow. Somehow we always think, "I can't quite do it now." What is the name of inadequacy? Tomorrow. And we have been doing that all of our lives. A challenge brings us to crisis; we feel inadequate to the challenge; we postpone. Then we live a life of being defeated — defeated by our own invention of time, our own assumption of inadequacy. What created all this? Thought, isn't it?

Thought would also say, "I can repeat the words of the lesson but I can't apply them." But this is a hypocritical statement. We are so casual we don't want to go further. We don't *really* want to change. "I want to *do* things. I want to be active. I want to improve myself." But there is a lack of passion to bring anything to application. When you harness the energy of truth, that very instant it is brought to application for the rest of your life.

So, we *want* the truth, but we don't want to bring it to application. And that's why we never have. Each person has to discover this. Then why preoccupy yourself? Why start a conflict in yourself? At least be aware of the deception. SEEING THE FALSE AS THE FALSE IS WHAT FREES ONE FROM THE FALSE. It awakens an awareness of the deception in which we are caught.

Don't feel helpless and say, "What am I going to do?" That sounds like thought speaking. Are you still listening to that? You just said, *These thoughts do not mean anything!*

So, we're neither here nor there. But we're going to be. Let's be glad about that. Just seeing the false as the false has its own action. The action of awareness is much stronger than the action of thought. Our only responsibility is to be honest.

What do you think awareness would do? When you say, "I agree that *these thoughts do not mean anything*, but I have responsibilities. I can't leave my job." —awareness would tell you that these are exactly the thoughts that keep you a slave. Then, awareness would continue to dissolve the thoughts on and on and make you aware that *these* thoughts do not mean anything either.

When you say, "What can I do?" awareness sees, "Look at the helplessness! It has exploited and manipulated me all my life." Awareness is the light that cannot be deceived. It is an awakening within oneself. But awareness doesn't tell you what to do. It only says, "See that what you're doing is false."

So then, what does awareness do? The action of awareness is that it undoes the activity of thought. Would you allow awareness to undo the things that you believe in — your misperceptions, your deceptions? Awareness, therefore, makes you more and more aware of the falseness of personal life, until you discover the only thing that is not false: the Will of God.

The Will of God has the vitality to take care of your making a living. It has the vitality to rotate the planets and move the oceans. It contains everything there is. We can see its supreme wisdom: the rhythm of the day and night and seasons, of your very heartbeat and circulation of blood. Everything. And would you not trust that? Would you rather trust in thoughts that do not mean anything?

If thoughts do not mean anything — and we just see through thought — then we cannot see anything. Everything has meaning but we've never seen it. We see nothing. When you *see*, in the true sense, you're no longer insecure, are you? You see the perfection that provides everything and you realize: "I understand nothing!" And you'll be back with the stillness.

It is important to learn to discover the virtues of stillness. Stillness can know reality; thought cannot. The stillness that knows reality tells thought what to do. Thought, then, would always express that which is of stillness, that which is eternal, that which is of God. But without the stillness we are only aware of the body and the body's senses; and the one thing we are sensitive to is sensation. And we always want more of it. Body senses can never know satisfaction. We have become a slave of physical sensation and therefore, constantly preoccupied with it.

Seeing this, you have a horror! There is no space in this preoccupation to be with silence. You realize: "I am in a prison and all that I'm concerned about is what sensation can do for me. There's no thoughtfulness in it, no love in it. All the time — sensation." In the absence of peace within, we are the slaves of sensation.

But being still, you discover that there is more than sensation in life. In this silence, in this boundlessness, there is pleasure in seeing the perfection of creation. Sometimes poets and artists have a glimpse of it when they make direct contact with the stillness of an object. They try to capture it in their poetry or paintings. The mystic, however, goes even further. He goes further and begins to outgrow it all.

And that's what we are to discover, so that conflict and duality may end. Somewhere we too have the dignity that is of the spirit. There is an inner calling, one's own function, that is one with the Will of God. When you have discovered that, you are at peace and you have something to give. Nothing external can affect a person who is related. He knows the truth of:

I am never upset for the reason I think.[6]

This lesson applies to everyone. Thus, the blessing is given to help us step out of all blame, all things that deprive us of peace. We are as God created us but the personality is what we have made. We are upset by our thought, but now we know that thoughts do not mean anything.

I am never upset for the reason I think.

The function of reason is to correct error. When you come to that reason, you are free from any error or mistake or misperception. Therefore, you would never be upset. Instantly you recognize that it is your interpretation upsetting you. Reason is a clarity that is *given*, a light which corrects whatever reactions are in you.

The lesson imparts the initiative to dispel illusions and allows you to no longer be dominated by those things that upset you. The minute a deception is dissolved, you are introduced to a miracle. The minute you see,

I am never upset for the reason I think.

there is the purity of space untouched by thought — a moment of eternity. You see how motives are always taking you away from it. Motives keep man active and busy; they have fear and ambition, desires and hate. This is what motives are made of and they never allow you to be who you *are*.

If you want to never be upset, then it is possible to bring this to application with the vibration of this lesson. It will simplify your life; it will change your lifestyle.

Read the lesson lovingly. It has the potential to free you from that which you *think* is happening to you externally. Nothing is. It brings everything to holiness and has the capacity to end separation and fragmentation. It brings you to a state of being untouched by thought.

It's easy to repeat the lesson — it's even easy to pretend we understand it — but the issue is still application. Without application it has no validity. Why is there not the application of the lesson? We know the words but why don't we want to know the fact of it? It is possible and it is an absolute necessity.

The Course is a joyous adventure and brings us to newness. You can't tell me you have learned the lesson if you are not with newness. Once understood, the learning I speak of is forever because it is not of thought. What would make us see this? What would bring about an urgency to see it?

> *I am upset because I see something*
> *that is not there.*[7]

Now that ought to make a real difference in your life!

To me, the other person is not external. Do you know what this means? It means that what a personality does in a body is not what you are going to relate with. He has a personality and idiosyncrasies, but that is not what you identify with. He is also eternal, created by God. This you could never know if you did not love the other person.

In the absence of not having the eyes to see the reality of who another is, we look upon the physical activity and label this good, this bad, and so forth. Don't we all do that? But love must go beyond that.

When we are not aware of who we are, we get deceived; we identify with our bodies and with our insecurities. Naturally, if we are to learn what love is, we will not identify with the body and personality. What a person does in a body is *not* real; what a person *is* is real. And what a person *is* is not a body.

Can you come to a living interest in which you want to know the truth of this? If so, you will call upon that potential within — the potential to receive. That is the action of *A Course In Miracles*. No greater blessing has ever been bestowed upon man than each lesson it contains.

We have to do the lessons in a very thorough way, for they are a process of awakening confidence and self-knowing. All that disturbs and deprives us of peace is to be looked at because, by nature, we are to be at peace. We *must* be at peace. Unless there is peace within, there will not be peace outside either. We are responsible for the wars and everything else that goes on in the external world. We have a responsibility not to add to the tension and friction. When you and I are at peace, something else happens externally also.

Silence draws to itself much more than we realize. Nothing else can offer what silence can. Yet we turn our back on it. And the lesson says:

My thoughts do not mean anything.[8]

This is such a significant lesson. How can we say these words and then give meaning to our thought? Silence helps one not to give value and importance to thought. It undoes thought's dominion over us. Everything is contained in this one lesson. It's a lesson one loves to read over and over again. It makes things so clear — if you are willing to give it the space. It frees you from all you now believe.

My thoughts do not mean anything.

I don't think any one of us disagrees with this in principle, yet somehow we can't let go. Just agreeing is not enough, however. We *have* to let go. At least we are becoming more aware.

What is it that gives thought meaning? Thought will not let go of thought even though it can agree it has no meaning. Are you grateful for the lesson that has brought this to your attention so clearly? You may say, "All right, I appreciate it. But I still can't let go." Perhaps if we were quiet and not so convinced that we are capable or incapable, we would come to inspiration. Out of inspiration something else may be born. The preoccupation with oneself drops away.

Become aware for a moment. Why go on giving meaning to: "I can't drop it," and continue to say: "*My thoughts do not mean anything?*" Not only are you not putting an end to your thought, you have added another phrase to your repertoire. And the lesson beautifully says: All right, if you can't let go, then just repeat this very slowly:

> *This idea will help to release me*
> *from all that I now believe.*

Doesn't that inspire you? It's like a guarantee, a promise. Can you accept that promise? It's a promise *He* is making. Have you read it that way? He Who is in charge of the process of Atonement is the One making this promise.

> *My thoughts do not mean anything.*

What happens when you take a moment to know your thoughts? Well, first of all, it brings you back to you — you're dealing with yourself and not with abstract thought. You're observing *yourself*; you become aware of your own thought.

If you are going to see the false as the false, start with seeing it inside yourself rather than outside. And that is where the miracle cuts time.

We can observe how little we are aware of our own thoughts. We are always aware of someone else's. Therefore, rather than to awareness, we give authority to the eyes that do not see beyond appearances and never awaken the inner eye, or inner awareness.

Can we see that thought relates me with the external and awareness relates me with my own thought? Do you see the difference? Instead of becoming aware of somebody else, I am now becoming aware of my own thought. "Know thyself" is taking place. I feel less helpless and less confused because I am dealing with just this. The only thing I have to deal with is my own thought.

You begin to learn more about yourself — your impulses, vested interests, what annoys or threatens you —but without any condemnation. Awareness eliminates judgment, whether the judgment is about you or a situation or another person. Do you realize that most of our "knowing" is judgment? It's not really knowing at all, but prejudice. The realization of this can bring about innumerable changes in our way of looking at things and in our thinking. Perhaps it would be a little easier to let go of our angry thoughts towards another, knowing,

My thoughts do not mean anything.

The observation of one's own thought and seeing the false as the false awakens us to discrimination. "My thoughts may not mean anything, but there must be another thought, the Thought of God." This realization keeps growing when the Course is read with a still mind. The Course has to be read with a still mind otherwise we are not reading it. It is the still mind that can say,

> My meaningless thoughts are showing me
> a meaningless world.[9]

Otherwise, it's a lie.

We read the Bible, the Koran, the Vedas — what difference does it make? Our lives are a contradiction to the truth they impart. Living in hypocrisy, we make a greater fool of ourselves. We know the words but we need to outgrow them. We will have to undo. Unless we have been silent, we won't know what undoing is; we just go on with the sensation of "knowing," the sensation of learning. Do you know what a trap that is? But that's sensation too, isn't it?

Stillness knows:

> My meaningless thoughts are showing me
> a meaningless world.

Unless we are still, we are not really reading it. The Course, then, becomes the heeding — the heeding that only silence can know, only stillness can know. Jesus said time and time again — and I'm sure every other person who had a still mind invariably said the same thing — "if you have the ears to hear."[10] We can't hear because we interpret. Interpretation is the activity of thought that distorts the hearing.

This is the eleventh lesson. We have been brought to a state where inner transformation takes place in eleven days. If we had been given this lesson on the seventh day we would not have been able to understand it in this particular way. It's not just a statement. It has the potential to transform one's life.

By the eleventh day, seeing the truth of it, one can be transformed. We really do recognize that these words of the Course have some semblance of truth in them. Less explaining is needed to make them clear. But if transformation is to take place, application has to be brought in — the application of really knowing the truth of it, not the intellectuality of it, not the words of it.

"The lesson is true but I am still caught in the meaningless world, and am still quite content with it." The two don't go together. We burn so much energy in distractions and indulgences and deviations. It's that same energy that is needed to bring about the transformation. Either the energy is dissipated in the activity of casualness or it is contained and you have the vitality that brings transformation. You can do it at any instant.

My meaningless thoughts are showing me a meaningless world.

What does this mean? It means you are not meaningless anymore because you are not of this world. If you see the world is meaningless, *you* must have become meaningful. And one human being who has become meaningful in a meaningless world is a benediction to the human race. Truth makes you meaningful. Receive the gift the lesson imparts.

I am upset because I see a meaningless world.[11]

We must go through this. You and I *are* the world. Then see how you are going to keep the upset going. "I shouldn't have done that. I'm going to do this." And right away one sees, "I'm back with my meaningless thoughts!" What does this? What brings this awareness that you are back with your meaningless thoughts? ...The still mind. The still mind silences everything.

The mania for learning is one thing that is silenced. Education has been one of the most detrimental things to humanity, because it merely trains people to fit into the system. Why should we be owned by anybody? If there were no insecurity and greed, you wouldn't want to accumulate more than another. There is such an abundance in Life. But where there is artificiality, there is greed.

There is another world — a world of peace, a world of holiness. That is our dwelling place. The still mind wants nothing of this world that's divided and lives by the dog-eat-dog approach. You are at peace and discover your needs are met. Nobody gave you the teeth, but as a child the teeth appeared. No system could have given you eyelashes. What was needed was provided. And you become part of that Intelligence, part of that action of Life.

A meaningless world engenders fear.[12]

If you are not part of the meaningless world — which is of thought — why then would you be afraid? What do you think insecurity is? Are we not all caught in it? We can't even afford to question it! "Who is going to look after us?" If we really knew our function, would that question arise? In the absence of knowing our real function, we become insecure and start a movement in our lives that is no longer related to reality. A wise person once said, "Make yourself a mule and someone will ride you." The lesson also says, however,

> *...a meaningless world is impossible.*
> *Nothing without meaning exists.*

The manmade world of beliefs, nationalism, armament, and so forth, is meaningless, but the world God created is not.

> *God did not create a meaningless world.*[13]

Isn't that beautiful? *God did not create a meaningless world* because now you see the world God created. It's a realization, a recognition of a fact; it's not just a phrase. If it is a phrase you're not with the world God created. *God did not create a meaningless world* means that you see what is meaningful, that which is of God, that which is eternal and does not change.

Then you discover:

> *My thoughts are images that I have made.*[14]

Your brothers have made the same images and they are caught in them, but you're not. You can make them aware of it: "I was a slave once too." What a function to show your brother that he is not blind! You help him remove the images.

And then you go further and come to:

God is in everything I see
because God is in my mind.[15]

One single truth in your life makes a tremendous difference. It changes your whole value system. But if we have not worked on the application of the lessons, then all of our intellectuality and all our "knowing" is utterly futile. In fact, it's an enemy.

The content, the source, of everything is God. But it is easier to say, "God is in this tree," than to say, "God is in this table," because the tree is alive and growing; it is part of the movement of Life. But as we said earlier, beauty is not in the object, it is in the seeing. And we've been stuck with the object. We have an opinion about it. If I like it, I want to own it; if I dislike it, I want to get rid of it.

Can you observe what part the activity of thought plays in your life — how much it dominates you? Why do you need opinion? Begin to discover: "I am nothing but opinion and I don't know how to exist without it." All right, then seeing the issue you can deal with it.

We have seen that thought has to be questioned and it can only be questioned by the state of serenity, or of stillness. Otherwise we get stimulated with our "knowing"; we are caught in the commotion of brain activity. But the mind is something else.

When you are in the *mind,* there is the seriousness and determination that does not deviate into the brain activity. In order to dissolve the latter, you have to come to that vitality in which there are no alternatives. Is that what you want more than anything else in your life? Otherwise it's merely readjustment at the level of brain activity.

Is this now clear, that the brain activity prevents you from knowing the God Who is in your mind? There is only one mind — the Mind of God. There is also only one brain. Each brain knows fear, has wants, is unfulfilled and conditioned. The brain has its limitations. It is attached to the body, to its personality.

The purpose of the brain, which is part of physicality, is to take care of the body. But we get preoccupied with the brain. One of its main characteristics is that it seems to always be in a state of unfulfillment. It always wants *more*. And it goes on accumulating until the day you die. Whatever it "learns," however, in the end must be unlearned.

The unfulfilled brain is never going to like silence; it is never going to like peace. But the silent mind is greater than the brain. Silence can observe; *it* can say:

God is in everything I see.[16]

Silence is the eye of God. It observes within and without. That which witnesses is not a movement of thought. Thoughts disappear just as darkness disappears with the coming of dawn. How gentle is its action! Could you convince the sun that there is darkness in the world? Something like that happens when one comes to a still mind.

Silence sees:

I am not the victim of the world I see.[17]

Silence is never the victim of the world because silence is not *of* the world. Unless silence is part of your life, you are still a victim of the world.

It is important to acknowledge and realize the fact of *what is*. Hunger, sleep, fear, and sex — these are common to everyone upon this planet. What distinguishes man from animals is his capacity to know God. Unless he has the knowledge of God, he is subject to what is timebound, to the law of survival. Thus each person remains isolated and tied to the personal.

Our "knowing" is limited to self and time. It is always of past or future. But there is a state in which fear is never experienced. And *A Course In Miracles* tries to awaken that yearning in us for what is real because what is real is already inherent in us.

The determining factor is our degree of receptivity. The issue was not that Jesus could not give truth — that's what He did — the issue was that out of thousands only eleven received it. Everything depends on our ability to receive.

We must read *A Course In Miracles* with receptivity because receptivity has the right relationship with truth. Receptivity awakens one's own potential; partial attention cannot — it remains at the level of brain activity, the level of relative knowledge, of our "knowings." We have to be with receptivity in order not to be a victim of the world. The choice is ours. It's not even a choice, it's a decision. You cannot put eternity into time, but you can put time into eternity and dissolve it.

> *I have invented the world I see.*[18]

What does it do to you when you read this? Mere intellectual knowing has no validity — other than its ability to invent a false world that doesn't exist. By now, this should be quite clear to us.

Religion is for those who are discontent with the false — the world of images and illusions. It is an action that refuses to be part of what is false. And *trying* to get out of it in itself is another illusion, for *trying* invents time. So you see, the lessons themselves are becoming quite confronting.

It is clearly stated in the *Text*,

> *Perfect love casts out fear.*
> *If fear exists,*
> *Then there is not perfect love.*

But,

> *Only perfect love exists.*
> *If there is fear,*
> *It produces a state that does not exist.*[19]

The lack of love has produced in us a state that does not exist. It is an escape from reality, from bliss even. And all we see is the manmade world, the world that is invented by ideas. That's the world we see. And we are convinced we can't survive without it. That's another invention. The root of it is fear. Survival is a projection of fear. And the Course says,

> Only perfect love exists.
> If there is fear,
> It produces a state that does not exist.

So, we have to deal with fear. But we *want* to be in a perfect state of love, which is again a wish and a wanting, another illusion. *We* have invented the fear; therefore, we can take care of it.

> You can give it up as easily as you made it up.[20]

What we have invented, we certainly can stop projecting.

> There is another way
> of looking at the world.[21]

All these lessons become truths. Right away you start putting away what thought is inventing. More and more stillness comes into your life and less and less words. We haven't yet known the power of stillness. The power of stillness knows that He Who created Life takes care of it.

> My mind is part of God's.
> I am very holy.[22]

Are you with the evolving process of Atonement as you read? If so, by the time you read this thirty-fifth lesson, you are as vast as the sky, taller than the stars. The sun and the moon you can hold in your palm. Your awareness is greater than the universe.

With Lesson 35, a great change takes place in the Course. It is a new beginning, a new discovery for those who have heeded the previous thirty-four lessons. To them, in particular, it is an important boon.

My mind is part of God's.
I am very holy.

can only be understood if we have done all that each day's lesson required. If the state of this lesson is not felt by the time we reach the thirty-fifth day, we probably haven't given the lessons the attention and integrity they demand. There is a beautiful Zen proverb which says, "When the archer misses the bull's-eye, he always finds the cause of the error in himself."

There should be great joy to realize the truth of this and to find out what prevented us from reading the thirty-four lessons. Why don't we know, *My mind is part of God's?* Could we ever want anything more? Do you feel that holy? What do we know if we don't know, *I am very holy?* Without the truth of it, life becomes a routine, a ritual.

My mind is part of God's, and so is yours. You are very holy. You can extend your sanity of fulfillment to the world caught in experience and the agony and bondage of unfulfillment. The world needs that. The world needs *you.*

Each of the thirty-four lessons of the Course has brought us closer and closer to the truth of Lesson 35. Every single lesson has taken away some corner of helplessness. Each has shown us clearly that we live in a psychological world of unreality, a world of ideas that are projected. Each has brought a release from the authority of thought over us and introduced us to the questioning of our conditioning. Each lesson has brought us to "Know thyself" in order to know:

> My mind is part of God's.
> I am very holy.

There should be great rejoicing in this. Yet somewhere we want to close that door of really knowing because we have a poor opinion of ourselves. There is resistance to knowing that which is True. This resistance has been inherent in man throughout the ages. Why are we resisting the knowing of, *My mind is part of God's. I am very holy?* The benediction of the lesson is still a stranger to us. Yet with every day's lesson, *He* comes to us. That discovery has to be made.

> My holiness envelops everything I see.[23]

We have difficulty believing that is who we are, let alone directly knowing it. Are we then really interested in Atonement — meaning the ending of separation — or is it just another wish and a wanting that could be put aside for something else?

> My holiness blesses the world.[24]

must be born out of a contact with the Reality of oneself. Is your holiness blessing the world? Do you believe it can? If *my holiness blesses the world*, what must I be?

There is nothing my holiness cannot do.[25]

Our first response to this is probably, "I wish that I *could!*" And there is a touch of doubt about it. Instead, can we ask, "If I can do everything, what is it that prevents me?" Can we see the power our conditioning has over us? What we believe has strong power. Do we see that? And that's the only thing that prevents it. "I am convinced I cannot do it."

This something called *you* cannot, but holiness certainly can. Man has been brought down to his personality, to physicality, to limitation. How indoctrinated we have become. One small deception, one small error, one small entry of thought — and look how many centuries upon centuries it has kept us blinded. We have become convinced of our littleness and we trust that that is true. If it can prevent us from knowing the truth of our holiness, then we have to admit that our conditioning has tremendous power over us.

Are we willing to face this as a fact? The problem is that we are self-convinced. Then once and for all we can understand one thing: the issue is not outside of me, the issue *is* me.

Just see what it would take to deal with your own doubt. If you could see this, you would probably relate with *A Course In Miracles* differently. This doubt that has beguiled you is part of your belief about yourself, your opinion about yourself. See how detrimental thought has been; it has deceived you. What vigilance would it take to never formulate a thought — knowing from the very outset that thought doesn't know, that it cannot know?

When you have seen the truth, there is only truth and not thought. Truth is that which is not touched by thought. We have lived by thought and now we must put thought away. The issue is thought versus holiness.

> *My holiness is my salvation.*[26]

> *I am blessed as a Son of God.*[27]

> *God goes with me wherever I go.*[28]

To be with the evolving process of Atonement is to come to the truth of Lesson 41. Before you start to read, ask help of Him Who is in charge of the process of Atonement. He has promised:

> *If it helps you,*
> *think of me holding your hand and leading you.*
> *And I assure you*
> *this will be no idle fantasy.*[29]

These are His words. Give them some space and then read the lesson knowing that He is with you. And He is. Everything becomes silent. Nothing is outside of that silence. It absorbs everything and brings it back to stillness.

> *God goes with me wherever I go.*

> *Today's idea will eventually overcome completely*
> *the sense of loneliness and abandonment all the*

separated ones experience. Depression is an inevitable consequence of separation. So are anxiety, worry, a deep sense of helplessness, misery, suffering and intense fear of loss.

The separated ones have invented many "cures" for what they believe to be "the ills of the world." But the one thing they do not do is to question the reality of the problem. Yet its effects cannot be cured because the problem is not real. The idea for today has the power to end all this foolishness forever. And foolishness it is, despite the serious and tragic forms it may take.

Deep within you is everything that is perfect, ready to radiate through you and out into the world. It will cure all sorrow and pain and fear and loss because it will heal the mind that thought these things were real, and suffered out of its allegiance to them.

You can never be deprived of your perfect holiness because its Source goes with you wherever you go. You can never suffer because the Source of all joy goes with you wherever you go. You can never be alone because the Source of all life goes with you wherever you go. Nothing can destroy your peace of mind because God goes with you wherever you go.[30]

If anything destroys your peace of mind it is because you have given it authority to do so. It's as simple as that. "I am giving authority to my thought that is depressing me. No one else is going to depress me or give me anxiety." Somewhere you and I are in charge. "I am a human being. I am the Son of God — not thought." Knowing this, you remain free of unloving thoughts.

Probably at some stage we need someone external to help us to undo our thought. That would be right education. But if that person is genuine he's going to make sure you don't become dependent on him. Neither will he form a religion or a clique. His job is undoing; therefore, he's not going to belong to anything. He is not going to say, "Do it this way or do it that way," but rather, "Look, you can do it. *You* begin to undo." The process of undoing, then, is essential for us to know.

And then you begin to understand the difference between *A Course In Miracles* and other scriptures. *A Course In Miracles* starts with undoing. You feel so blessed that it has come, that *you* are the one to whom this gift has been given, that,

God goes with me wherever I go.

You are no longer alone. You have a relationship with the Course and you have a friend — a friend, a brother, the Light of the world Who has taken charge of the process of Atonement and given you *A Course In Miracles*. You see the compassion of Heaven, that you and I are part of the Will of God. And you value that blessing.

Nothing can destroy your peace of mind because God goes with you wherever you go.

We understand that you do not believe all this. How could you, when the truth is hidden deep within, under a heavy cloud of insane thoughts, dense and obscuring, yet representing all you see?[31]

Now, who is going to listen to insane thoughts? If we have heard what the Course is saying, any time insane thoughts come up you can dissolve them. The stillness would know what is insane because stillness never gives power to insanity. That's why it is always still. And then an action begins of which we know nothing as yet. But it will unfold.

Today we will make our first real attempt to get past this dark and heavy cloud, and to go through it to the light beyond.

There will be only one long practice period today. In the morning, as soon as you get up if possible, sit quietly for some three to five minutes, with your eyes closed. At the beginning of the practice period, repeat today's idea very slowly. Then make no effort to think of anything. Try, instead, to get a sense of turning inward, past all the idle thoughts of the world. Try to enter very deeply into your own mind, keeping it clear of any thoughts that might divert your attention.

From time to time, you may repeat the idea if you find it helpful. But most of all, try to sink down and inward, away from the world and all the foolish thoughts of the world. You are trying to reach past all these things. You are trying to leave appearances and approach reality.

It is quite possible to reach God. In fact it is very easy, because it is the most natural thing in the world. You might even say it is the only natural thing in the world. The way will open, if you believe that it is possible. This exercise can bring very startling results even the first time it is attempted, and sooner or later it is always successful. We will go into more detail about this kind of practice as we go along. But it will never fail completely, and instant success is possible.

Throughout the day use today's idea often, repeating it very slowly, preferably with eyes closed. Think of what you are saying; what the words mean. Concentrate on the holiness that they imply about you; on the unfailing companionship that is yours; on the complete protection that surrounds you.

You can indeed afford to laugh at fear thoughts, remembering that God goes with you wherever you go.[32]

The first response of the brain is always fear, suspicion, doubt — some inadequacy. Try it out. It's a fact.

What is your response to this lesson, *God goes with me wherever I go,* if you have really heard it? It could be a kind of thank you, a joyous feeling that's eternal because God's Thought is eternal. Can we say a "thank you" that's eternal? Can we say "thank you" with our real thought, with God's Thought? Someone who really says "thank you" will ever be with God.

How few words we have ever uttered in our lives that were eternal! *My thoughts do not mean anything.* It's good to be aware of that, isn't it?

Another thing about this lesson we should be aware of is that it is a description of what meditation is. Meditation is a state of innocence that can say, "I don't know." It is the greatest gift of God. Thought doesn't know. Therefore, it's free. The brain becomes the potential when it is empty of thought. And out of that a new expression is born. It is new because it's not projected, it's not personal. And what is new? The new is dropping the falseness of personal life and being part of all Life.

So, spend some time and get to know this lesson. You will find that *God goes with me wherever I go* — from the meaningless thought within, to a place of quiet in which nothing is separated, where everything is whole. If you take that journey, you are blessed. There is no other journey.

We have the gift of *A Course In Miracles.* Each day all our questions, all doubt, all suspicion, all confusion, all that thought distorts, can be silenced and cleansed and brought to a different state.

What a benediction to be born at the time of the Course. Learn to respect and to love what is true. Enrich yourself with the glory of the truth, and with the blessing of what it offers.

PART THREE

3

WHAT IS FORGIVENESS?

*F*ORGIVENESS RECOGNIZES *what you thought your brother did to you has not occurred. It does not pardon sins and make them real. It sees there was no sin. And in that view are all your sins forgiven. What is sin, except a false idea about God's Son? Forgiveness merely sees its falsity, and therefore lets it go. What then is free to take its place is now the Will of God.*

An unforgiving thought is one which makes a judgment that it will not raise to doubt, although it is not true. The mind is closed, and will not be released. The thought protects projection, tightening its chains, so that distortions are more veiled and more obscure; less easily accessible to doubt, and further kept from reason. What can come between a fixed projection and the aim that it has chosen as its wanted goal?

An unforgiving thought does many things. In frantic action it pursues its goal, twisting and overturning what it sees as interfering with its chosen path. Distortion is its purpose, and the means by which it would accomplish it as well. It sets about its furious attempts to smash reality, without concern for anything that would appear to pose a contradiction to its point of view.

Forgiveness, on the other hand, is still, and quietly does nothing. It offends no aspect of reality, nor seeks to twist it to appearances it likes. It merely looks, and waits, and judges not. He who would not forgive must judge, for he must justify his failure to forgive. But he who would forgive himself must learn to welcome truth exactly as it is.

Do nothing, then, and let forgiveness show you what to do, through Him Who is your Guide, your Savior and Protector, strong in hope, and certain of your ultimate success. He has forgiven you already, for such is His function, given Him by God. Now must you share His function, and forgive whom He has saved, whose sinlessness He sees, and whom He honors as the Son of God.[1]

* * *

Forgiveness recognizes what you thought
your brother did to you has not occurred.

In order to know this, it is obvious that you have to be in a totally different state of being — a state that has no alternatives to truth in it, a state that doesn't have duality in it. Otherwise, what we call forgiveness is but another point of view and therefore, still of relative knowledge.

Forgiveness itself is Absolute because it does not accept anything that your brother did as real — that at the level of truth, at the level of love, at the level of reality, it never took place. Forgiveness never becomes involved. This means, then, that you have to be so awakened that you would not deceive yourself. It is a different state.

Now, when we say we understand what forgiveness is, can we see that our understanding is just of relative knowledge? Can we see that at the thought level we will never succeed in forgiving? What if you and I really began to see that at the thought level we can dislike someone and then forgive them, but that both are just temporary? Tomorrow the person may again do something I don't like, and again I am going to become non-forgiving.

So then, I am the one who is regulated by the unreality of the externals that do not exist. Therefore I must first come to terms with my own self, deal with my own inadequacies, my own misperceptions, and discover I cannot forgive because I do not know love. Intellectual forgiveness is not love; it is a substitute.

Knowing this awakens the recognition in me that there is another state of being of which I am capable of becoming aware — if I so choose. But at my present level of casualness — part indifferent, part helpless — I have a vested interest in what I believe in, and when you do not agree with me, we clash.

When men live by this kind of thinking they produce a civilization of conformity. They worship authority and indoctrinate people; they live under the authority of the "head man."

Man has lived throughout the ages without knowing what forgiveness really is. It is something vast; it civilizes a person. Forgiveness takes him to a much higher level of being; it plays an essential part in freeing him from all deceptions. And the action starts within himself.

If we are unforgiving, the outcome is war. We have a vested interest in something and are always thinking about ourselves. If we could only see that our vested interest is our bondage! When others do not agree with us, we accuse them. This kind of life is a torment because it has no love in it. To know forgiveness is to know liberation. Without forgiveness, there can never be freedom.

> Forgiveness recognizes what you thought
> your brother did to you has not occurred.
> It does not pardon sins and make them real.

When you forgive the way you do, "Oh, never mind, I forgive you," you are still giving reality to what you think that person did. But, *forgiveness recognizes*. This is seeing with a different kind of eyes. It is a state within you that you recognize, a state which is no longer offended, no longer a slave of anything. You recognize that within you is a reality, a clarity, a vitality that is independent. And that reality or vitality is ever present in you. You may come upon what is known as the Grace of God, the action of Love, the source of Life. When you are related with this, then this is what you extend, and forgiveness is in effect.

If you have understood the word "forgiveness" and the word "recognition," you don't need to read or learn anything else. You can have a dozen PhD's, but if you cannot recognize who you are or what your original state is, then your education has been merely an indulgence and a distraction. It prevents you from recognizing the truth where conflict and separation end.

The word "recognition" in itself is quite confronting. What have we ever recognized? At a lower level, I "recognize" you as a bad man because you don't believe in my dogma. Isn't it? But true recognition means that you recognize we are inseparable beings because we are part of the same Life, we breathe the same air. To recognize that! It is something that comes to liberate you, to bring you to your natural state of love and non-separation. This you *recognize;* it is not learned. In that moment an awakening takes place in you. What a gift you have given to yourself! And that is the gift you extend.

Forgiveness does not mean that somebody has done you wrong and you blame them and then say, "I forgive you." Jesus, when crucified, said:

"FORGIVE THEM;
FOR THEY KNOW NOT WHAT THEY DO."[2]

He was not a party to what someone else did. He was independent. Of what? He was independent of reaction. Life is creative. Life is an action; and action is always an extension of Love. It is independent; it doesn't react. This is the purpose of man on earth — to extend what is eternal, not what is of time and vested interest.

When you recognize that part within you — something true in you — you discover peace and you extend peace. What a joy for the awakened man to do nothing other than to extend forgiveness. What would that state be? To extend forgiveness is to no longer have vested interest. Nothing owns you but you have something to give to the whole planet, to the universe.

It does not pardon sins and make them real.
It sees there was no sin.

Isn't that much better? Forgiveness does not acknowledge sin as real because, in the one who forgives, that separation never took place. The word "sin," according to *A Course In Miracles*, means "separation"; and the word "atonement" means "where the separation has ended." Whatever is separated has no reality. The Introduction to the Course states:

Nothing real can be threatened.
Nothing unreal exists.

And forgiveness remains steadfast with that. It is never deceived.

It sees there was no sin.
And in that view are all your sins forgiven.

All right. So now, what are we regulated by? We are regulated by the belief that: "If I am separated, then I have to struggle for my survival. I have to get locks and keys." And with the mechanism of defending and protecting, a totally different activity begins.

When you are not separated, however, all this is gone. You liberate yourself from those things. If you are not attached to anything, you are not going to get offended. When you are no longer fragmented, does it matter to you what the other person's nationality is, or what denomination he belongs to?

What is sin,
except a false idea about God's Son?

We have to see that the forgiveness we know is only an *idea*. Are we listening carefully to what the Course is saying, that every idea is false? Can you give me an idea that is not false? We think ideas are real but ideas only came into being when the extension of what you are ended. When you are isolated and separated, you move from separation, and ideas assume a reality, non-forgiveness assumes a reality, so-called "sin" assumes a reality, even though in actuality, they do not exist.

That actuality is what you and I have to recognize. Recognizing actuality is what truth is. There is a vast difference between idea and truth. What is that difference? Truth is unchangeable for it is Absolute; ideas are ever changing. What is of God, what is of the Son of God, is Absolute and therefore not subject to time or circumstances. It does not change! You can crucify Jesus, He is not going to change. He is not subject to the projections by which we live.

> *What is sin,*
> *except a false idea about God's Son?*

So then, continually, I think you are wicked because you have supposedly done something that I judge to be wrong. You might have been hungry and stolen a loaf of bread. According to our laws of "me and mine," that needs punishment. Yet one wonders if that bread, that wheat, the earth in which it grew, the sunshine and water that made it grow, belongs to you. It belongs to that which does not change. And it is extended, it is given. How many misperceptions need to be undone just to recognize the truth or to learn what forgiveness is.

One lesson of *A Course In Miracles* can totally liberate you because every word, every line has a miracle and a revelation in it. You begin to see with the eyes of the Holy Spirit Who accompanies you when you read it. Without His help you won't understand the truth the Course imparts.

How open we have to be! But you say, "Open? I am pressured by time. While I'm reading, I'm also thinking about something else." And if one pushes a little further, the person will inevitably say, "How am I going to survive? I have a job!" All these justifications, all these excuses — and the Course is asking us why we don't want to raise them to question?

If you could raise them to question, miracles would undo them for you. You would have a clearer vision and, step by step, you would begin to come to your own light. It is this light that recognizes. It is the light within you that recognizes the truth as the truth and sees the false as the false. Even the question of forgiveness does not arise if that correction is made within, because there is no other; there is only the One Life.

> *What is sin,*
> *except a false idea about God's Son?*
> *Forgiveness merely sees its falsity,*
> *and therefore let's it go.*

Can you see something as false? If you see it as false, does it have any existence? What state are you in when you see it? Would you not feel relieved, liberated? And there are no efforts in it. Are you delighted by that, that it requires no effort? You see the false as the false and it is gone! That's all you have to do — to see the false as the false.

Why is it that we can't see the false as the false? The Course gives us the answer in a prayer from the *Text* when it says we are asleep.

> *The sleep of forgetfulness is only*
> *the unwillingness to remember*
> *Your forgiveness and Your Love.*[3]

Therefore, you and I have a responsibility to first recognize that we are asleep. Because we divide everything, we don't see reality. How beautifully the Course puts this:

> The sleep of forgetfulness is only
> the unwillingness to remember
> Your forgiveness and Your love.

You and I have to discover the meaning of this unwillingness that rules our lives. As long as that is not dealt with we will never know the truth of forgiveness. The only issue is the unwillingness, isn't it? Somewhere we have our conclusions; we think we are weak, confused; we don't know what to do; we become helpless and justify; and we believe everything we interpret. Thus the unwillingness to be awakened continues — generation after generation.

> What is sin,
> except a false idea about God's Son?
> Forgiveness merely sees its falsity,
> and therefore lets it go.
> What then is free to take its place
> is now the Will of God.

The Course uses a very beautiful expression here, "God's Son." The Son of God is the one you want to forgive. But unless you yourself are the Son of God, you won't know what forgiveness is. And if you are God's Son, what would you know? ...The Will of God.

> *What then is free to take its place*
> *is now the Will of God.*

You start extending the Will of God. The Will of God is indivisible. It is not divided. Everything that exists is part of its extension; that is its energy; that is its reality.

> *An unforgiving thought is one*
> *which makes a judgment*
> *that it will not raise to doubt,*
> *although it is not true.*

Why don't we see that we can't raise it to doubt because we are asleep? There is an unwillingness and a lack of energy, a lack of passion. Yet we have the energy for destruction. We have the energy to punish. That takes energy too! Look at all the prisons. Look at the pain in the world because man knows to punish and not to forgive. Isn't that what wars are about? It has been from the beginning of time and it goes on more and more. We live by the law of punishment. Are you going to step out of it? You want to forgive intellectually, but you can't forgive as long as you are living by the law of punishment. And the whole world is on fire with hate and armament. But man cannot survive without forgiveness.

What power a man has who can turn the cheek! He is not attached. He is outside time, outside reaction. One such man could change the destiny of a nation no matter where he is in the world. Because he does not live by the false law of punishment, the heavenly powers are behind him. And this is something you and I can do.

About the law of punishment, there is not much we can do but see the false as the false. We want to change other people. But you can only change other people when you don't live by the law of judgment or the law of punishment. You'll change other people because you are extending love. *Wanting* to change them is an action of inadequacy; it's an idea. In the extension of love, there is truth and it extends itself. It is never a part of what is of time, nor does it believe in punishment.

Each one of us has the potential to come to that action but we want to be with forgiveness as a part-time thing, "I forgive you. Oh, I am so happy!" Is it possible for a mundane person to forgive anyone if he is still living by, "I forgive"? Where there is "me and mine," can there be forgiveness? Is forgiveness possible where there is duality? Is forgiveness a relative state? Is forgiveness personal?

What would you recognize if you could really forgive? You would recognize that the only problem in the world is man's problem with man. All problems exist in relationship. That is where the friction is. We don't have a problem with the moon or with the waves of the sea, nor with the songs of birds or the rivers that flow. The problem only comes in when you say, "This is mine," and I say, "No, it's mine." How powerful are the forces of "me and mine." And as a result, we have invented all kinds of systems by which to punish.

> *An unforgiving thought is one*
> *which makes a judgment*
> *that it will not raise to doubt...*

So then, what is this unwillingness that will not raise a judgment to doubt? There is something you and I have to *do*. But we want some guru to do it for us. And the gurus sell their relative knowledge and make you dependent on them. Then they exploit you and give you interpretations about that. Isn't it?

What are you going to do about your insanity? Have you seen by now that a non-forgiving state is an extension of insanity? You have to do something within yourself. It is an internal issue. Why is there the unwillingness to take care of your insanity? Why is there this irresponsibility?

We are trying to focus the attention on the fact that the action begins when the one who is reading this book has started to make the correction within himself. When unwillingness is gone, responsibility has dawned. Without responsibility, no one can be free.

You are responsible for what you do, for what you think. When you are irresponsible you are part of the multitude, the collective consciousness which knows nothing of love or forgiveness. It is ruled by nationalism, by one dogma and belief system after another. It doesn't think. And *A Course In Miracles* says, yes, that is so, but the individual can step out of it. That individual is *you*.

You are important. Society will not change but the human being can. A human being is one who has no grudge against another; a citizen has a grudge against another citizen because they are both programmed and conditioned. A human being is not conditioned; he lives by the law of forgiveness, by the law of Grace. Anyone who does not forgive lives by the law of punishment, by the law of judgment, the law of separation, the law of fear. Yet it is given to man to rise above that and be as God created him.

> *An unforgiving thought is one*
> *which makes a judgment*
> *that it will not raise to doubt,*
> *although it is not true.*

A *Course In Miracles* helps you when you make a judgment. The Course brings it to your attention: "Look what you are doing." And it undoes it for you. It undoes misperceptions and liberates you.

The teacher, then, is your own awareness, your own ability to recognize the truth. Every person is blessed with that. No matter how wicked you think someone else is, the memory of God is still in him. There is a part of him that is as perfect now as when he was created. That perfection is protected and guarded by Divine Forces. No one in the world walks without that light, without that perfection. It is at the level of "doings" — where we think the other should conform to our opinions and our wants — that we go astray.

To see the holiness of Life is to have reverence for Life. To see the holiness in the other! What peace you have just seeing that. You are blessed with having the eyes to see.

Seeing your brother introduces you either to your own holiness or to your own judgment. The Course says that

when you make a judgment a   iracle can free you from
it — not by "learning," but just by saying: "Is that true?
...Is that true?" Truth — which is within you — liberates
you the minute you raise the judgment to question.

An unforgiving thought is one
which makes a judgment
that it will not raise to doubt,
although it is not true.

You see, we don't really care for truth, do we? Our
judgment is not truth but we go on with it. Now tell me,
what other lessons do you need? Once you have seen it
is not true, can you drop it? And if you did, would you
not feel boundless?

Somewhere man must have cried with a great
yearning, "I wish I knew how!" *A Course In Miracles* is the
how. That is the action of Grace. It is the action of Life itself
that extends itself and says, "I will help you." *A Course In
Miracles* is the direct Thought of God — a gift given to
His Son. Would you receive it? Would you accept it?

What greater gift could the Father give to His Son? The
gift of miracles and revelations; the gift of the Holy Spirit
to liberate him from his misperceptions, from his own
deceptions and wrong-mindedness.

Let us see if we can read the Course that way now and
listen to it very carefully. What is it that is being pointed
out? Do we *know* the state of the word the Course is
talking about or do we just know it as an idea? That is our
responsibility.

*An unforgiving thought is one
which makes a judgment
that it will not raise to doubt...*

Are you going to be willing now? That you will never make a judgment? Will you make that demand of yourself never to accept unwillingness as real? All of mankind is enriched by your action of letting go of unwillingness and judgment.

I will not accept your unwillingness as real. Out of this intimacy and love for truth, it is possible for you and I to invite the strength and support whereby we can share what is of God. This is not me giving to you, or you giving to me, but rather the receiving for both. Once we have received what is of God; we become custodians for all mankind and then we pass it on.

The Name of God has its own vitality. It can save the world; it can save you too. Insecurity is outgrown in a flash. Fear is gone. And we are no longer regulated by survival.

*An unforgiving thought is one
which makes a judgment
that it will not raise to doubt,
although it is not true.*

Are we beginning to see that as long as we are unwilling, we will not raise it to question? That is the issue you and I have to deal with. Why is it we will not raise it to question? Why are we so indifferent? Why is there this unwillingness?

A Course In Miracles is to be brought to application, not merely be learned. Its purpose is not intellectual learning. It is to be lived! It changes one's whole lifestyle. It affirms:

> *I will not value what is valueless.*[4]

Then you and I are transformed.

> *The mind is closed, and will not be released.*
> *The thought protects projection,*
> *tightening its chains...*

The mind is closed... What do you think nationalism is? Is it not a tribal approach? *The mind is closed...* and we can't let go of our prejudice against our fellow man. Both sides think the other side is wrong. With the modern media and printed magazines and newspapers, what do you think is happening to man? More chains, more fear, more insecurity, more hate. What are *you* going to do about that?

> *The mind is closed, and will not be released.*

If someone tells you something that goes contrary to what your belief system is, you'll burn inside, won't you? We don't want to see the falseness of it and so we become defensive, we get hurt. We are not taught to look upon man as part of the One Life we share with Him. We are taught to live under this flag or that flag. That is the way of the collective. But the individual doesn't have to live this way.

Can you, as an individual, then say, "I see my mind is closed. I don't want to open it because I'm afraid." Unless you do, you'll continue with the fear. Do you want to live in your own fear or do you want to be liberated from it? That is the question. Where there is fear, there is also non-forgiveness.

And what did the Master say?

"I SAY UNTO YOU, LOVE YOUR ENEMIES."[5]

Not just one another, but your enemies also, because at the level of forgiveness or Love, there are no enemies at all. And what are most countries doing now? Every country has an enemy. People they have never met or even seen — but they are now their enemy.

> *The mind is closed, and will not be released.*
> *The thought protects projection,*
> *tightening its chains, so that distortions*
> *are more veiled and more obscure...*

This is our state of being when we do not open the closed mind. And we want to find out: why is it that the mind is closed and we prefer to leave it that way? You would say, "I don't have the vitality. I don't know what to do." And I would ask you, "How do you dissipate your energy? Is what you are doing meaningless? Is it essential? Is it born out of insecurity?"

This kind of questioning will bring about a different order, a different lifestyle. Raise these questions and say, "I want these things dissolved." You can then find out: yes, miracles work! Don't accept what anyone tells you.

Find out. Once the miracle has taken place, it is your own direct experience.

So, will you raise questions, knowing that the mind is closed? Have you come to the conviction that you are not going to live with a closed mind anymore so that you don't become *more* unwilling? This is a step we have to take. We have to raise questions so that we can come in contact with the miracle this Course is about. Then something beyond the miracle takes place—a revelation, a greater span of light.

> *The thought protects projection,*
> *tightening its chains, so that distortions*
> *are more veiled and more obscure;*
> *less easily accessible to doubt,*
> *and further kept from reason.*

If you remain unwilling, then you are going to leave those things intact. As long as you want to leave them there, there will be the incompleteness. You will want to "learn" more. But the fact is, you can't "learn" more; you can only undo, you can only unlearn. If someone shoots you with an arrow, you want the arrow taken out, don't you? You don't say, "Put another three in there." It is the learning, by which we are conditioned and programmed, that needs to come out. The awakening would want to raise questions. And if you don't raise questions, you are not a student of the Course.

> *What can come between a fixed projection*
> *and the aim that it has chosen*

as its wanted goal?
An unforgiving thought does many things.

Please begin to see that when you are non-forgiving, you are poisoning your blood. How much energy it takes! Constant preoccupation! Collectively, that hate becomes rampant in newspapers and magazines. And nations start manufacturing the deadliest of weapons. We *have* to take care of that poison within.

An unforgiving thought does many things.
In frantic action it pursues its goal,
twisting and overturning what it sees
as interfering with its chosen path.

That chosen path is something you are responsible for. It is your conclusion, is it not? And your conclusion is based on the idea of fear, survival, or helplessness. This is what we have to undo. Is there such a thing as fear and insecurity in the God-created world, or do they exist only at the level of ideas? Don't you want to know the truth? I am not saying it is one or the other; *you* have to find out what the truth is. Otherwise you merely change your opinion and nothing has happened.

Distortion is its purpose,
and the means by which
it would accomplish it as well.
It sets about its furious attempts
to smash reality...

Isn't that what we do? Do we not have furious attacks within us when we don't forgive? Wherever there is judgment, there are furious attacks. Look at what the world is producing with these furious attacks: it costs thirty million dollars to manufacture a war plane. Thirty million dollars — and there is hunger in the world. There are mental institutions, prisons; the old people are abandoned, children rejected. "Go. Learn. Take care of yourself. Get yourself a job!" The pressure of time!

Then you express your frustration through distractions — from one gratification to another, from smoking to drinking. Begin to see the insanity of it all. Is there any morality left? Is there anything honest in one's life? We are constantly running away from ourselves — anything to gratify.

What if you really knew the love that is in you? What if you recognized the joy within you, the peace within you? Would you be so scattered?

> *It sets about its furious attempts*
> *to smash reality...*

You are smashing your own reality. The Course is not talking about something external. It is talking to *you*, your reality, your God-given nature!

> *It sets about its furious attempts*
> *to smash reality...*

Are we not doing that all day? That's what most lives have become — *furious attempts to smash reality*. Fear becomes real and there is the daily routine of doing something unessential, sitting in an office where you become a mercenary! *Furious attempts* — that is what is alive. People stuck to jobs, having lost their own intrinsic work. This is a civilization of mercenaries furiously smashing their own reality. But you will not be satisfied; you will not be content with your littleness.

There is a section in the *Text* which begins:

Littleness Versus Magnitude

> *Be not content with littleness. But be sure you understand what littleness is, and why you could never be content with it.*[6]

Do you want to understand littleness? The wise always undoes. And that is why such a wise one as Socrates was poisoned to death, and Jesus crucified. The wise begins to undo your littleness and tries to introduce you to your boundlessness. And the whole system, based on vested interest, gets threatened. It is "safer" to be little and smash reality, but you will not be content. No one can be content with self-deception.

> *Littleness is the offering you give yourself. You offer this in place of magnitude, and you accept it. Everything in this world is little because it is a world made out of littleness, in the strange belief that littleness can content you.*[7]

Are you going to raise that to doubt, that littleness can content you? Or are you satisfied being little, caught in the routine of doing the same thing over and over again? A mercenary!

When you strive for anything in this world in the belief that it will bring you peace, you are belittling yourself and blinding yourself to glory. Littleness and glory are the choices open to your striving and your vigilance. You will always choose one at the expense of the other.[8]

So there you are. We are either responsible or we are irresponsible. That is a decision each person has to make. If you make the decision, you will raise questions about *littleness*, you won't raise questions about more "learning." But that's for sale, isn't it? Misperceptions whereby you feel a sense of lack. "Learning" is of littleness. A real teacher, a friend, can only make you more and more aware and help you to recognize, "Look, you are honoring littleness. It doesn't exist." He is not doing anything other than to say, "Look at this."

So, you see the false and it drops away. You continue to recognize until you are freed from your self-deception. And the world changes. A few people... Jesus only had twelve and look what they accomplished.

We come back to *What Is Forgiveness?*

*It sets about its furious attempts
to smash reality,
without concern for anything
that would appear to pose a contradiction
to its point of view.*

All points of view are mental. Truth cannot fit into a point of view. Where there is truth, there is reality and it is not manmade. Points of view are manmade and have no reality. Truth is of God and it does not change.

> Forgiveness, on the other hand,
> is still, and quietly does nothing.

Can you imagine what stillness would be? A still mind!

A still mind is at peace.
A still mind is an awakened mind.
A still mind is part of God.

The activity of the brain is silenced. It is cleansed of all reaction, all judgment, all forgiveness and non-forgiveness. It is out of it all.

> It offends no aspect of reality,
> nor seeks to twist it
> to appearances it likes.

Do you twist things to the appearances you like? Begin to recognize that when the Course describes what sanity is, it is not something we know. We only know to manipulate and to twist. Have you ever come to a still mind? Try it for five minutes and see if you succeed. You'll find out how conditioned you are.

> It merely looks, and waits, and judges not.

What a sight that must be! It waits. It is still. And *it merely looks*. Every deception dissolves itself before the light of that stillness. You are freed from activities and you become an extension of the Kingdom of God on earth.

He who would not forgive must judge,
for he must justify his failure to forgive.

How are we going to justify our failure to forgive? We can get very enthusiastic and say, "Oh yes, I forgive this one, I forgive that one." That's as far as we go, isn't it? But who will accept it when it is a deception? That which changes, that which is of time, is not real. It is just a ritual of your own deception.

What would it take to really know the truth of forgiveness? What would it take? A total change of lifestyle. We want to do it gradually and therefore validate there is a tomorrow, there is time. And back again we are with deception.

But he who would forgive himself
must learn to welcome truth exactly as it is.

Have you ever seen truth *exactly as it is?* Is the human brain capable of seeing anything *exactly as it is?* That which is *exactly as it is* is not subject to time. We look at human relationship and see he or she is good or bad, and so forth. But that is not *exactly as it is.* It is but a psychological view of our own and has no reality.

Do nothing, then,
and let forgiveness show you what to do...

Would you allow the power of forgiveness to transform and cleanse you? Would you be weak if you knew forgiveness? Would you be little? Would you close your mind to a power mightier than all of creation? Do you take forgiveness for weakness, for an idea?

If you know what forgiveness is, you are the master of all that is created. Everything in creation bows to you, to your perfection, to the love and blessing you bring to this planet.

Do nothing, then,
and let forgiveness show you what to do...

When you do, you will know what vitality you have. You are not little. When you feel little, you are drafted into some nonsensical function, some paper work, producing unessential things. How can you be happy then? You need outlets. And that is what most of our energy and money goes into. To sustain non-forgiveness is a torment worse than any hell the Course ever pictured.

Do nothing, then,
and let forgiveness show you what to do,
through Him Who is your Guide,
your Savior and Protector...

Accept no one else as your Guide and Savior. Everyone else is your brother. Have that discrimination and relate with the Teacher Who gave you the Thoughts of God. He is in charge of the process of Atonement. He is the Son of God because He is part of the One Mind. There is only the One Mind. He wants to introduce you to that and not make you any less than who He is. You become part of the only Reality, the same One Mind, the Mind of God.

He has never deviated from God-Consciousness. He extends only that. And you too will extend only that. Would you rather have littleness or be what God created you?

Do nothing, then,
and let forgiveness show you what to do...

We always want to know what to do. We always think there is someone who will tell us. That's the way we were brought up; we are programmed. "Somebody is going to tell me what to do." Will you heed forgiveness, let *it* tell you what to do?

What would forgiveness tell you to do? It will tell you to forgive, to put away your punishment. You will say, "I like forgiveness, but I am not going to give up punishment. I know my views about so and so." There is always the giving up.

Learn from forgiveness. What will forgiveness teach you? No teacher, no school, no university could teach you in a million years what forgiveness can teach you in five minutes. We have gotten caught in this deception of educated ignorance — the schools and the training and the skills that have deceived man, and that promote the concept of punishment too.

Forgiveness is not a meek thing, "I forgive you." It is for people who are alive and honest, untouched by what is unreal. Forgiveness is untouched by falseness. It is a light unto itself.

Do nothing, then...

Is it possible for you to do nothing? We don't have the space! We are enclosed; our heads are crowded. There is no space between the thoughts! There is no space to be silent! When there is, we quickly want to run. The space is taken away from us; we are working like slaves from morning to evening just for survival.

Where is the space — the space to be yourself, not to be a citizen? You'll most likely end up in jail if you want to have your own space. We are bought and sold! We have no claim to our own life! Have you ever realized how programmed and conditioned we are? There is no space to step out of it and see the falseness of it. We'd rather keep our mind closed to it and merely talk about forgiveness as if it were something sentimental. Forgiveness is a lifestyle that relates man with Eternal Laws, not manmade rules.

Do nothing, then,
and let forgiveness show you what to do,
through Him Who is your Guide,
your Savior and Protector,
strong in hope,
and certain of your ultimate success.

Are you ever certain of anything? At the level of change, is there certainty? If you were certain, would you not be strong? Certainty cannot be taken over by profit and gain at the expense of someone else.

Forgiveness is a certainty. Time cannot touch it; no one can regulate it. It is who you are in reality. Forgiveness is an expression of Love. Love is real, fear is not. Fear makes man little. Love liberates.

> *He has forgiven you already,*
> *for such is His function,*
> *given Him by God.*

So then, you don't have to worry about punishment. Once you forgive, you also learn that you were forgiven for whatever you thought you did. "What a sinner I am. What wrong things I did." Only at the level of illusions do they occur. At the level of reality, they never have. You are out of it all. You are as God created you.

> *I am not a body. I am free.*
> *For I am still as God created me.*[9]

It is not something you have to achieve; it is something you recognize and realize.

> *Now must you share His function,*
> *and forgive whom He has saved...*

Now you want to forgive your brothers and you have a function in life. *You* have a function in life and the Heavens surround you. Your function is the one thing mankind needs and thirsts for! To free man from the bondage of his own "knowings," from his fears, his hate, his conditioning. Just as a flower is a flower and it has its own fragrance, you stay with being just you.

Being yourself brings the Kingdom of God to earth and then forgiveness teaches you what to do. You become a co-creator with God — He Who never punishes, Who doesn't acknowledge there is sin or guilt, no nationalism, no fear of survival. You begin to extend that which does not change, that which liberates you and therefore, liberates your brother. You no longer see any separation between you and your brother. It is a total change of your state of being. It is not a change of ideas, for ideas have no meaning. But you have changed; you have realized your own Identity.

> *Now must you share his function,*
> *and forgive whom He has saved,*
> *whose sinlessness He sees,*
> *and whom He honors as the Son of God.*

To know that God only sees the sinlessness in you gives you energy. Out of the gratefulness and joy of your heart, you extend your blessing and your love for your brother. Love is the only thing you and I can share.

Thank you and God bless you.

PART FOUR

4

THE LESSON OF THE DAY

How WONDERFUL IT IS to sit quiet. Somehow one steps out of the darkness of the world and rises higher and higher till one is in a totally different state. It makes one even independent of the body. This is what silence imparts, those moments of stillness. The body no longer intrudes; it is content, at peace. One could sit for hours without moving. The activity of the brain comes to stillness, as if everything has been settled. There is no anxiety at all; nothing is unresolved. Rather, there is something else — the unknown, the wordless. The brain doesn't try to understand it because it is beyond its reach. It finds great joy in humility and in discovering the innocence of non-activity. You would never think that the brain could make that discovery, but it does. And then it is purified, silenced. Not by imposing silence; it just becomes silent.

Then, out of non-interference, you begin to see with eyes that are not of the physical senses. The seeing we know can go as far as that wall and then it is blocked. Or the seeing can go as far as our opinions and ideas, and then it is blocked. But in silence, all of that ceases and you discover how boundless and holy man really is.

As long as the brain is without that holiness, it feels like an orphan. It resorts to seeking, wanting, groping, — hoping it can gratify, satisfy, complete itself. But the incompleteness continues. There is no real satisfaction in it. It remains dependent on the externals.

The state we speak of knows nothing as external because it relates with everything. There is no conflict in it; everything is included in it. The externals are never real except to the brain that is caught in illusion.

Sitting quiet introduces one to that. However, we get caught, not in silence, but in the activity of getting to silence. The minute you think about it with the brain, you get caught in the externals that are not real. And hardly anyone sees the paradox of it. Seeking thus becomes important. But if there is seeking, you haven't got it. The seeking can only take you away from that state because it is an activity, and stillness is non-activity. That's quite simple.

Lesson 242 of *A Course In Miracles* is:

> *This day is God's.*
> *It is my gift to Him.*[1]

What does this really mean? What gift would one give to God? What gift do you think God wants? You can't give Him the moon and you can't give Him flowers. What would you give?

According to the lesson, this is the day which you have given to God. *This is my gift to Him.* The obvious question is: what would you give? We can read the lesson casually — *This day is God's. It is my gift to Him.* — and it won't mean anything. We have a tendency of doing it just that way; we think that because we have muttered the words, we have read it. Nothing seems to make a change in us. We can read the Bible or the Koran, whatever, but it doesn't really bring about a change. We think change comes with effort and struggle. "I've got to do this. I've got to do that." We're not present enough to see that "doing" is again activity.

How can you say, *This day is God's?* This lesson is a challenge. Indeed, each lesson is a challenge. What do you think when you read it? And that's just the problem, isn't it, because the minute you start thinking about it, you are blocked and blinded by the thinking. The minute you resort to thinking, you've gone astray, because then you are not with *this day* — you're with a million yesterdays.

Thinking is the echo of yesterday. Therefore, you can't give Him *this day.* You have filled it with your echoes. *This day* can only be given when your mind is absolutely still, when nothing intrudes upon it. Then you can say,

This day is God's.
It is my gift to Him.

"I cannot give Him something that is an object but I can give Him my stillness." When you are not preoccupied with something else, you have given Him a gift. How simple! How direct! But today, anything that is simple and direct has become very difficult for man. It has become difficult because the anxiety and preoccupation are constant — during sleep, driving a car, eating — it goes on and on.

This day is God's means that you have no projections, no images, no errands. Can we afford to give one minute to this? This is not to say that you are not going to eat or go to the bathroom. If you have to sneeze, you don't have to control it. These are body needs and they're simply met. They don't interfere.

So now we are seeing something very beautiful: the body's needs are direct. Hunger is direct; you don't have to go to school to learn anything about it. If you want to sneeze; you sneeze. Pain is direct; you know what to do. Put your hand on a hot stove and you'll take it off quickly. The body knows what to do. It has its own intelligence. There's no philosophy in it. It's direct and you can meet it directly.

To make the body's needs psychological is a fallacy and a deception. The problem comes in when we try to impose something upon ourselves — meditation, with its fixed pose, for example — because it is then of our own images. I'm saying that if there is a seeking for something, you haven't gotten it. I'm talking about "having" it, not "seeking" it.

We have settled the body issue, that when the body is hungry, it's hungry; when it's hot, it's hot; and you know what to do. So, the body's needs for the day are met — we have enough water to drink and food to eat; there is heat and comfort in our homes.

So then, can we give the day to God? Obviously, it is not the body He wants. He wants your stillness so that He can communicate with you. Our anxiety about the body — which is of survival — prevents us from giving the day to God. One day. If we succeeded in giving a day to God, we would never be alone again.

When I discover directly that I am never alone, then my anxieties are gone. My day is full of gladness. And I bring about:

"THY WILL BE DONE IN EARTH
AS IT IS IN HEAVEN."[2]

I come to another peace, totally independent of "me and mine," of the psychological confusion and the seeking and the wanting.

Body needs are direct and nature takes care of them. Where there is a need, that need is already met. It took billions of years for this planet to prepare for the entry of mankind. When man entered, the temperature was right, the water was pure, the streams were running, the birds were singing. There was great beauty upon the land. All this to prepare for the Son of God to walk the earth! Everything was provided, and is still provided in spite of our profiteering corporations.

Giving one day means not letting yesterday intrude. That's all. It is bringing an end to what is dead, the past. The past is never in the present. The present is here and we are always absent. And this is our day not to be absent.

Each day's lesson has so much to impart.

> *This day is God's.*
> *It is my gift to Him.*

Just the joy of being able to give a gift. You begin to understand that love is the most precious of all that is. Out of love emerged all manifestation. Out of love you and I were created. Love is what God is; and what He is, is what we are. Only God could give this gift — totally, wholly, timelessly, forever. The power of love can do anything. It can part the sea. Anything is possible with love.

Originally, man could tell the tree to bear fruit and it would. Man could endow power to any plant or leaf, and thereby heal his fellow man. We have lost all that. We have substituted it for the power of physics and chemistry and weapons. But this is not power; this is madness. The power of love has been replaced with the power of fear. It is you and I who are in the grip of fear. You and I are responsible for our own anxiety — it is not somebody "outside." We all have the same traits whether we are Hebrew or Hindu, Moslem or Christian. Which one of us is free of anger? And what makes anger Jewish and not Moslem? It's all so silly. Anger is anger; it has no religion or nationality. Fear is fear. See the comedy of the human being who thinks the other person has the "bad" and he's got the "good."

Why blame other people? Inside of you is where the correction has to take place. And once it's corrected there, no one is outside of you. You see that man is the altar of God, although he has become confused and misled — like you and I have been confused and misled. We have made everything psychological. We know so much *about* everything, yet we don't know anything.

Do you know the miracle of a finger or a drop of blood? What can you say as a fact, as a truth? Truth encompasses everything, don't you see? Nothing is outside of truth. But the truth we know is that the Mexicans are this way and the Canadians are that way. This is not truth — it is just opinion and prejudice. As long as we are caught in prejudices and opinions about others, are we any better than those we are condemning?

This day is God's.
It is my gift to Him.
I will not lead my life alone today.

Isn't that beautiful? You see, the moment you and I get down to the brain level, we are isolated from one another and "I'm alone" becomes a fact. Once I'm alone, I'm concerned about survival and I watch out for the one who stands in my way. And as the population increases, the competition gets stronger and we are getting more and more isolated.

I will not lead my life alone today.

Could you say this? You have to; this is today's lesson. Do you have a voice that can say so and mean it? Or do we say something and not mean it? Would this not be decadence? Can you say,

I will not lead my life alone today?

Would you turn your back on God or away from that stillness? Most of us want to be in that Presence. But nevertheless, our priority is still ourselves, our preoccupations.

Why are we so defeated? Why do we have such poor opinions of ourselves? Invariably you'll think you have to do something. When you go towards doing something, you're going to be defeated — at the level of activity and doing, you're finished. But if you come to stillness, then nothing of thought can intrude upon it. There is no comparison, no inadequacy, no ambition, no wanting, because stillness has that wholeness.

Man is part of the action of fulfillment, not the activity of unfulfillment which is always seeking, always wanting. We need to be touched by that fulfillment. More and more, each generation is misled and educated just for survival. We have a responsibility to leave behind a different world for our children. Where are the people who will leave behind something wiser? Where are those who can say: "Listen, it took me years but I finally woke up. And now I'm going to leave behind a wisdom that will cut time, a wisdom that will eliminate deception?" Then you have made a contribution. You have helped another so that he doesn't have to go through fifty years of ignorance and illusions because you did. What greater gift could you give than to reduce the external anxiety and bring a child to his own holiness?

Are not the older people of today irresponsible for the most part? What wisdom do they have to leave behind? The TVs have gotten them. As for the rest of us, we waste so much time because we don't know what to do. Indulgence has become important. That is inevitable when you do work that's unessential. When you do work that doesn't sing to you, you need to unwind and outlets become important. Where is the wise person who will make us aware of this? There are Marlboro signs all over the place — buy this whiskey, buy that cigarette. Billions of dollars are spent on publicity and advertising. Simplicity is gone. What a cursed thing is this affluence. It is as cursed as poverty.

> *I will not lead my life alone today. I do not understand the world and so to try to lead my life alone must be but foolishness. But there is One Who knows all that is best for me...*

And Who is this One? It would have to be someone like Christ — someone who is whole, not someone who is divided; someone who knows no yesterdays or tomorrows, who is as vast as the present. The present is limitless and this limitless state is within us.

There is One Who knows all that is best for me...

Don't you want to get to know that? To know *what is best for me!* If you were ever to pray, what would you pray for? Obviously, not for things. If God doesn't want the moon, why should you want the moon or a mountain or a ranch? Why? What would you want? ...That which is best for you — freedom from attachment. Have you ever prayed for that? It's not a wanting at all. And then you have the One Who would help you get it.

If you want "things," then you go to the earth to get them. If you want a state, you have to turn to Heaven. Heaven is of the Love of God. It is a State of Being, not a place. As a place, there is no heaven; as a place, there is no hell. Where there is an opposite, it is never real.

> *There is One Who knows all that is best for me and He is glad to make no choice for me but the one that leads to God.*

No choice — that's freedom! If you are really interested in saying, *this day is God's,* then you have to put the choices away. Right there is the freedom. Once you have dissolved the choices, or conquered the choices, or understood the choices, you are free of them.

So, the lesson provides the vitality, the insight. Insight shows you that without choice there is no wanting; choice is but conflict; choice ties man down to deception and to the earth. That's the key.

*And He is glad to make no choice for me
but the one that leads to God.*

How beautiful! We think we can't live without choice.
It's a "free country" because I can choose what I like. But
what I choose and what I like may not be consistent with
what *leads to God.*

Since you are giving the day to God as a gift, obviously
you would want a lesson that would help you to do so.
So there is consistency. You can be grateful that the keys
are imparted in the lesson of the day. Insight is given.

*I give this day to Him
for I would not delay my coming home.*

There is urgency. The minute you come to urgency,
you are getting closer to the NOW. A casual mind would
never know Heaven, would never know serenity.
Casualness is a breeding ground for images, choices, and
desires — like a swamp for mosquitoes. And there is
urgency because this is "the day." In one day you can
liberate yourself. *I would not delay my coming home.* But
our "home" is not of that state — our "home" is: "I want
this. I want that." We are so attracted to the things of the
earth — things that are manmade and not God-created.
And we can't even see that the manmade things are, for
the most part, an exploitation of what God created, from
which we make money. If we would only see the cruelty
of man upon man. Where is reverence for Life?

And it is He Who knows the way to God.

The One Who knows the way to God! You are not alone because He is with you. You are part of the same spirit. Christ is a State. There was a man named Jesus Who, while in His personality, realized the State and became the Christ. The Christ State exists in each one of us, in you. Why then are you behaving as a personality?

Each person is the Christ. If you have given the day to God, you may see others as the Christ and not as an idiosyncrasy, irrespective of what they do. And you would feel blessed.

This day is God's.
It is my gift to Him.

And it becomes "my" gift to "you," for you are of God. You are an extension of God.

Then the prayer begins:

And so we give this day to You.

He Who is the Christ is with you. He is holding you by the hand and together you are saying this prayer.

And so we give this day to You.

...to God. He is no longer far away because when you come to the present, He is right there. It is the same vibrant State.

We come with wholly open minds.

You couldn't go to Him any other way. Now you are clarifying what has brought you there.

> *We do not ask for anything...*

Goodness gracious! No more choices — not even for nirvana! That's all finished.

> *We do not ask for anything*
> *that we may think we want.*

Wanting only exists when there is thought.

> *Give us what You would have received by us.*

Now, the two who are saying this — the Christ and you — are asking God, *Give us what YOU would have received by us.* You can only give back love. And "Love ye one another" becomes the one, sole function of life upon this planet. When I give love to you, I'm also giving it to God.

> *You know all our desires and our wants.*
> *And You will give us everything we need*
> *in helping us to find the way to You.*

We certainly don't need desires; we certainly don't have anything to wish and want for. The only want is to find the way to Him, or to your own Identity. Man has ignored this essential issue and nothing else is going to bring peace to him or to the world. Peace is not external.

I am saying that you and I have to assume responsibility. We have to want to go home to that State of Oneness in which there is a sharing of love. Politicians are not going to seek love; they're going to talk about peace and seek war because the industrial economy thrives on it. Knowing this, you and I have a responsibility to find peace within ourselves. Then we can give that peace to a brother. If you can't find it, don't expect someone else to find it for you. Deadlier weapons, bigger warships, faster missiles — none of these are going to do it. There is no love in it.

This day is God's. It is my gift to Him. — brings me to stillness. Whatever I do out of this stillness no longer disturbs the stillness. The body can move because it has its own needs, but it doesn't disturb the stillness. And I never make a problem of anything because there are no problems in life. Problems are projected.

In reality, all is good. There is such gladness in one's heart when "all is good" becomes real and is not just an idea. All is good — there is no more seeking and you are at peace.

That goodness exists in every person. How sad that we are oblivious to it. Just imagine what you would see, knowing that all is good. Never would your life be touched by a choice. We are caught in preferences because we are not aware that all is good. Once you are with "all is good," you will see the wisdom of the state that accompanies it. Once you see that "all is good," then you are with the wisdom of that state. And that is God's gift to His Son.

Wisdom is superior to choices and goodness brings gladness into one's heart. This you can share with someone else who thinks goodness doesn't exist. What a thing is, is what it extends. If you're worried, you extend worry. But if there is goodness, it also extends itself. And then you can respond to the need of a brother because you have no need of your own. That is the function of a minister of God.

A Course In Miracles prepares each one who is with it to finally become the minister of God. That becomes one's own last function. One might say, "How can I become a minister of God? I'm ignorant." But the Course points out that if you are sincere, then whatever inadequacies you have will be taken care of as you start helping others with theirs.

There is a lovely prayer in the *Text* which reads:

I am here only to be truly helpful.

These are strong words. *I am here ONLY...* That makes it whole. It can't be partial, otherwise it's an idea or an ideal, and they both create conflict.

I am here to represent Him Who sent me.

He Who sent you is ever with you. If your words are honest, an awakening takes place and you go beyond the words.

I do not have to worry...

It is you who are saying this. You're not just repeating the words. The minute you're here *only* to represent Him Who sent you, you will realize it.

> *I do not have to worry*
> *about what to say or what to do*
> *because He Who sent me will direct me.*

All is over, isn't it? There is no need to accumulate a lot of information and ideas. And the freer you are, the more you are giving your day to God. We think the only thing that matters is skills and techniques — the "how to" of the age of destruction.

> *...He Who sent me will direct me.*

He becomes you, the separation ends, and you are at peace. The mind must come to stillness. You don't have to go back to the brain to think about it; you are part of God's Mind. You extend His Thought.

> *I am content to be wherever He wishes...*

How nice! No more duality, no more choices. *I am content.* As long as there are choices and "wantings," we will never know what contentment is. Contentment is a state within one and it knows peace.

> *I am content to be wherever He wishes...*

That is true devotion, true purity. That is the verticalness of man.

I am content to be wherever He wishes
knowing He goes there with me.

You are always surrounded by the peace of Heaven, by the joy of Life — for Life is joyous. It is not for problems.

I will be healed...

Granted there are inadequacies, but listen to what He says:

I will be healed
as I let Him teach me to heal.

So, we have to heal in order to be healed. Therefore, to love another is the only way. Love only knows the One Life. There is no "other" in love. All fragmentation ends. When reactions cease in man, he is part of the Kingdom of God. Who can say, "I have come to step out of time and its reactions and illusions to know what is eternal?" Who can say, "I have come to make my will one with God's?"

There is every reason to be glad and joyous. It is your intent that makes it work.

CONCLUSION

How one relates with the daily lesson of the Course is of utmost importance. Unless one's own energy is blended with intensity of interest, one will be able to give neither reverence nor the quiet space within. Mere reading will not realize the Truth of the Thoughts of God the lesson contains. We insist that the Course is to be lived, not theorized.

The serious student of *A Course In Miracles* no longer lives by assumptions — he values what is Eternal, and for this, wholeheartedness is required.

Will you bring deceptions to an end in your life? Is not the undoing of deceptions the first function of responsibility? We cannot justify our being taken over by the externals without imposing or validating the weaknesses within us. Yet weaknesses are not real.

This realization is the breakthrough the earnest student of *A Course In Miracles* has to make to be an extension of the Mind of God. It is mandatory that the student go past learning to make it his own conviction. Only then will he know his own holiness.

ADDENDA

THE PATH OF VIRTUE

THE PURPOSE of the Foundation for Life Action
is to be with the Eternal Laws
so that it does not become and organization.

LOVE IS ETERNAL.
ABILITIES EXTENDING LOVE ARE BLESSED.

In the absence of Love
abilities become the bondage of skills,
limited to personality.
Among virtuous men,
it is what the human being IS that is Real,
and not what he does in a body.

The purpose of the Foundation is to be part of

GOD'S PLAN FOR SALVATION.[1]

Thus it has a difference point of reference
than the thought system of man.

Obviously, the Name of God
cannot be commercialized.
There are no fees in what we share.
We do not believe in loss and gain.
Non-commercialized action is provided by
the blessings of productive life.

"IN GOD WE TRUST"

Those who are with the Eternal Laws
in times of change remain unaffected.
In crisis, it is your care for another
that is your strength.

We have a function in the world
to be truly helpful to others,
knowing:

I am sustained by the Love of God.[2]

My only function is the one God gave me.[3]

Nothing real can be threatened.
Nothing unreal exists.[4]

We are not pressured by the brutality of success.
We are blessed by the work we do.
Gratefulness is complete, as love is independent.

To us, you, the human being, come first.
Thus it enables us to go past

the conventional opinion of right an wrong
and relate directly to you.

For man is as God created him,
unchanged by the changeable society
that rules his body with its belief systems.

The Truth is a Fact that dissolves illusions of time.
Our function is to dispel the abstraction of ideas
and realize the actuality of Fact.

For,

> *I am under no laws but God's.*[5]

Reverence for Life is of a still mind
hallowed by His Love.
This transformation is what we call

THE PATH OF VIRTUE.

The Path of Virtue is the ministry of gratefulness.

The wise who extends the Kingdom of God on earth
lives consistent with,

"BUT SEEK YE FIRST THE KINGDOM OF GOD,
AND HIS RIGHTEOUSNESS;
AND ALL THINGS SHALL BE ADDED UNTO YOU."[6]

BIOGRAPHY
TARA SINGH

TARA SINGH IS KNOWN as a teacher, author, poet, and humanitarian. The early years of his life were spent in a small village in Punjab, India. From this sheltered environment his family then traveled and lived in Europe and Central America. At twenty-two, his search for Truth led him to the Himalayas where he lived for four years as an ascetic. During this period he outgrew conventional religion; he discovered that a mind conditioned by religious or secular beliefs is always limited.

In his next phase of growth he responded to the poverty of India through participation in that country's postwar industrialization and international affairs. He became a close friend of Prime Minister Nehru as well as Eleanor Roosevelt.

It was in the 1950's, as he outgrew his involvement with political and economic systems, that Mr. Singh was inspired by his association with Mr. J. Krishnamurti and the teacher of the Dalai Lama. He discovered that mankind's problems cannot be solved externally. Subsequently, he became more and more removed from worldly affairs and devoted several years of his life to the study and practice of yoga. The discipline imparted through yoga helped make possible a three year period of silent retreat in Carmel, California, in the early 1970's.

As he emerged from the years of silence in 1976, he came into contact with *A Course In Miracles*. Its impact on him was profound. He recognized its unique contribution as a scripture and saw it as the answer to man's urgent need for direct contact with Truth. There followed a close relationship with the Scribe of *A Course In Miracles*. The Course has been the focal point of his life ever since.

Mr. Singh's love of the Course has inspired him to share it in workshops and retreats throughout the United States. He recognizes and presents the Course as Thoughts of God and correlates it with the great spiritual teachings and religions of the world. From Easter 1983 to Easter 1984, Mr. Singh conducted the One Year Non-Commercialized Retreat: A Serious Study of *A Course In Miracles*. It was an unprecedented, in-depth exploration of the Course. No tuition was charged.

Mr. Singh continues to work closely with serious students under the sponsorship of the Foundation for Life Action, a school for bringing *A Course In Miracles* into application and for training teachers of *A Course In Miracles*. He is the author of numerous books and has been featured on many audio and videotapes in which he discusses the action of bringing one's life into order, freeing oneself from past conditioning, and living the principles of the Course. He offers two regularly scheduled retreats on *A Course In Miracles* annually: New Years and Easter.

REFERENCES

INTRODUCTION TO THE SECOND EDITION

1. *A Course In Miracles* (ACIM), first published in 1976 by the Foundation for Inner Peace, Tiburon, California, is a contemporary scripture which deals with the psychological/spiritual issues facing man today. It consists of three volumes: *Text* (I), *Workbook For Students* (II), and *Manual For Teachers* (III). The *Text*, 622 pages, sets forth the concepts on which the thought system of the Course is based. The *Workbook For Students*, 478 pages, is designed to make possible the application of the concepts presented in the *Text* and consists of three hundred and sixty-five lessons, one for each day of the year. The *Manual For Teachers*, 88 pages, provides answers to some of the basic questions a student of the Course might ask and defines many of the terms used in the *Text*. (Editor)

2. The Scribe of *A Course In Miracles* asked why the Course was being given at this time, and was told: "The world situation is worsening to an alarming degree. People all over the world are being called on to help, and are making their individual contributions as part of an overall prearranged plan. Part of the plan is taking down *A Course In Miracles*, and I am fulfilling my part in the agreement, as you will fulfill yours. You will be using abilities you developed long ago, and which you are not really ready to use again. Because of the acute

emergency, however, the usual slow, evolutionary process is being by-passed in what might best be described as a 'celestial speed-up.'" See *Journey Without Distance: The Story Behind A Course In Miracles* by Robert Skutch (Celestial Arts, 1984), page 60.

3. ACIM, I, Introduction.
4. ACIM, II, page 3.
5. ACIM, II, page 16.
6. ACIM, II, page 25.
7. ACIM, II, page 50.
8. ACIM, II, page 55.
9. ACIM, II, page 63.
10. ACIM, II, page 31.
11. ACIM, II, page 174.
12. ACIM, II, page 177.
13. From Thoreau's *Walden: Or, Life In The Woods*, first published in 1854. (Editor)
14. ACIM, I, page 5.
15. ACIM, I, page 49.
16. ACIM, II, page 162.
17. ACIM, II, page 396.
18. ACIM, II, page 213.
19. "In God We Trust" appears to have been inspired by a line from *The Star Spangled Banner*, "In God is our trust," written by Francis Scott Key in 1814. "In God We Trust" first appeared on the coinage of the United States in 1864, during the presidency of Abraham Lincoln. It became the official motto of the United State in 1956. (Editor)
20. ACIM, I, page 326.
21. Ibid.
22. See ACIM, I, pages 426-427; II, page 120 and following. (Editor)
23. ACIM, II, page 32.
24. See reference no.2.
25. ACIM, I, page 444.
26. ACIM, III, page 10.
27. Refers to Matthew 13:13-23.

28. Refers to the song, "The Seventy," first sung at the Forty Days in the Wilderness Retreat. See Tara Singh's *The Voice That Precedes Thought* (Foundation for Life Action, 1987), pages 282-283. (Editor)
29. ACIM, I, page 464.
30. ACIM, I, Introduction.
31. John 5:30.
32. See ACIM, I, pages 208 and 210; II, page 120.
33. ACIM, II, page 162.
34. Refers to Matthew 18:20.
35. ACIM, II, page 283.
36. Refers to: *The journey to God is merely the reawakening of the knowledge of where you are always, and what you are forever. It is a journey without distance to a goal that has never changed.* See ACIM, I, page 139.

FOREWORD

1. ACIM, I, Introduction.

INTRODUCTION

1. ACIM, II, page 290.

PART ONE: HOW TO LEARN FROM
A COURSE IN MIRACLES

1. ACIM, I, page 430.
2. ACIM, I, Introduction.
3. ACIM, II, page 112.
4. ACIM, II, page 3.
5. Ibid.
6. ACIM, I, page 253.
7. ACIM, II, page 376.
8. ACIM, II, page 392.
9. ACIM, II, page 154.
10. Matthew 11:15.
11. ACIM, II, page 13.

12. ACIM, II, page 15.
13. ACIM, II, page 16.
14. Ibid.
15. Ibid.
16. ACIM, II, page 18.
17. ACIM, II, page 21.
18. ACIM, II, page 23.
19. ACIM, II, page 25.
20. Ibid.
21. Ibid.
22. ACIM, I, page 464.
23. ACIM, I, page 418.
24. ACIM, II, page 432.
25. Matthew 6:10.
26. ACIM, II, page 119.
27. ACIM, II, page 189.
28. ACIM, II, page 174.
29. ACIM, II, page 172.
30. ACIM, II, page 384.
31. Ibid.
32. ACIM, II, page 384.
33. Ibid.
34. Ibid.
35. ACIM, II, 214, page 384.
36. Ibid.
37. ACIM, II, page 79.
38. ACIM, II, page 395.
39. ACIM, II, page 229.
40. ACIM, I, page 442.
41. ACIM, I, page 444.
42. ACIM, I, pages 460-461.
43. ACIM, I, page 468.
44. ACIM, I, page 466.
45. ACIM, I, pages 476-477.
46. John 13:34.
47. ACIM, I, page 109.

PART TWO: THE FIRST FORTY LESSONS

1. ACIM, II, page 3.
2. ACIM, II, page 4.
3. Refers to: *I* [the Author of the Course] *am in charge of the process of Atonement, which I undertook to begin. When you offer a miracle to any of my brothers, you do it to yourself and me....When you have been restored to the recognition of your original state, you naturally become part of the Atonement yourself.* See ACIM, I, page 6. (Editor)
4. ACIM, II, page 5.
5. ACIM, II, page 6.
6. ACIM, II, page 8.
7. ACIM, II, page 10.
8. ACIM, II, page 16.
9. ACIM, II, page 18.
10. Refers to Matthew 13:13-17.
11. ACIM, II, page 19.
12. ACIM, II, page 21.
13. ACIM, II, page 23.
14. ACIM, II, page 25.
15. ACIM, II, page 47.
16. ACIM, II, page 45.
17. ACIM, II, page 48.
18. ACIM, II, page 49.
19. ACIM, I, page 12.
20. ACIM, II, page 49.
21. ACIM, II, page 50.
22. ACIM, II, page 53.
23. ACIM, II, page 55.
24. ACIM, II, page 56.
25. ACIM, II, page 58.
26. ACIM, II, page 60.
27. ACIM, II, page 62.
28. ACIM, II, page 63.
29. ACIM, II, page 119.
30. ACIM, II, page 63.
31. Ibid.
32. Op. cit., pages 63-64.

PART THREE: *WHAT IS FORGIVENESS?*

1. ACIM, II, page 391. In Part II of the *Workbook For Students* the lessons are interspersed with *"...themes of special relevance." What is forgiveness?* is the first of these themes.
2. Luke 23:34.
3. ACIM, I, page 326. The prayer which contains these lines has been referred to as *A Course In Miracles'* version of the Lord's Prayer. See: *Journey Without Distance: The Story Behind A Course In Miracles* by Robert Skutch (Celestial Arts, 1984), page 68. This prayer is discussed in great detail in *Dialogues On A Course In Miracles* by Tara Singh (Life Action Press, 1987), pages 35-167. (Editor)
4. ACIM, II, page 239.
5. Matthew 6:44.
6. ACIM, I, page 285.
7. Ibid.
8. Ibid.
9. ACIM, II, page 376.

PART FOUR: THE LESSON OF THE DAY

1. ACIM, II, page 404.
2. Matthew 6:10.

ADDENDA: THE PATH OF VIRTUE

1. See ACIM, I, pages 426-427; II, page 120 and following.
2. ACIM, II, page 79.
3. ACIM, II, page 107.
4. ACIM, I, Introduction.
5. ACIM, II, page 132.
6. Matthew 6:33.

OTHER MATERIALS BY TARA SINGH RELATED TO *A COURSE IN MIRACLES*

BOOKS

Dialogues On A Course In Miracles
"Love Holds No Grievances" — The Ending Of Attack
How To Raise A Child Of God
The Voice That Precedes Thought
A Course In Miracles — A Gift For All Mankind
Commentaries On A Course In Miracles
The Future Of Mankind — The Branching Of The Road

AUDIO CASSETTE TAPES

A Course In Miracles Explorations
The Heart Of Forgiveness
Bringing A Course In Miracles Into Application
"What Is The Christ?"
Discussions On A Course In Miracles
What Is A Course In Miracles?
Freedom From Belief
Discovering Your Own Holiness
Raising A Child For The New Age
Finding Peace Within
Discovering Your Life's Work
Tara Singh Tapes of the One Year Non-Commercialized
    Retreat: A Serious Study of *A Course In Miracles*

VIDEO CASSETTE TAPES

"Give Me Your Blessing, Holy Son Of God"
"If I Defend Myself I Am Attacked"
Our Story — What Led To The One Year
　　Non-Commercialized Retreat?
"Do Only That" — A Course In Miracles And
　　Working With Children
"Nothing Real Can Be Threatened" — A Workshop On
　　A Course In Miracles
　　Part I　　 *— The Question And The Holy Instant*
　　Part II　　*— The Deception Of Learning*
　　Part III　 *— Transcending The Body Senses*
　　Part IV　 *— Awakening To Self Knowledge*
Finding Your Inner Calling
How To Raise A Child Of God
Exploring A Course In Miracles (series)
　　— What Is A Course In Miracles?
　　　and "The Certain Are Perfectly Calm"
　　— God Does Not Judge and *Healing Relationships*
　　— Man's Contemporary Issues
　　　and Life Without Consequences
　　— Principles and *Gratefulness*
A Call to Wisdom
　　and *A Call to Wisdom — Exploring A Course In Miracles*
Man's Struggle For Freedom From The Past
　　and *"Beyond This World There Is A World I Want"*
Life For Life
　　and *Moneymaking Is Inconsistent With Life Forces*
The Call To Wisdom: A Discussion On A Course In Miracles
"Quest Four" with Damien Simpson and Stacie Hunt
"Odyssey" and *"At One With"* with Keith Berwick

———————

Book and tape catalogues available from:

LIFE ACTION PRESS
902 South Burnside Avenue
Los Angeles, CA 90036